Kerry Explains
The Law of Attraction

Are you ready for a life upgrade?

KERRY LAWS

With illustrations by Matteo Reggi

BALBOA.PRESS
A DIVISION OF HAY HOUSE

Balboa Press books may be ordered through booksellers or by contacting:

Balboa Press
A Division of Hay House
1663 Liberty Drive
Bloomington, IN 47403
www.balboapress.co.uk
1 (877) 407-4847

Because of the dynamic nature of the Internet, any web addresses or
links contained in this book may have changed since publication and
may no longer be valid. The views expressed in this work are solely those
of the author and do not necessarily reflect the views of the publisher,
and the publisher hereby disclaims any responsibility for them.

The author of this book does not dispense medical advice or prescribe
the use of any technique as a form of treatment for physical, emotional,
or medical problems without the advice of a physician, either directly
or indirectly. The intent of the author is only to offer information
of a general nature to help you in your quest for emotional and
spiritual well-being. In the event you use any of the information in
this book for yourself, which is your constitutional right, the author
and the publisher assume no responsibility for your actions.

Print information available on the last page.

ISBN: 978-1-9822-8167-0 (sc)
ISBN: 978-1-9822-8168-7 (e)

Balboa Press rev. date: 06/26/2020

For the cutest little Mamie, le petit maman, thank you for walking alongside me in this life, thank you for being my rock, my hero, and for making me who I am.

For Matteo, the man of my dreams, thank you for these beautiful illustrations, and all of the love, support, and happiness that you've brought into my life.

For Kalisha, my believing mirror, who supports me in all that I do, who talked with me at length about the content of this book, and who inspires me every day.

For all of the people who have crossed my path and taught me so much along the way, thank you for your love, your time, your presence, and your lessons.

Chapter One

MY STORY

Do what you want. There aren't any grownups around.
If you want to eat cake for breakfast you can.

I WAS A GROWN up from an early age. The circumstances I was born into as an only child of a soon to be single mum, from a poor background, experiencing periods of homelessness and financial struggle, prepared me to focus on survival, to put others first, and be a responsible mini adult long before many others tend to be. I was a tough cookie, hardy and dependable. My mum and I worked together as a team to survive the hardships we faced. We took on the responsibilities together.

The childhood I experienced was what it was, it made me who I am, able to face any crisis without panicking, wise beyond my years, and happy with my lot no matter how much that was. I was blessed in a way, but also cursed with issues I had to work through later in life as I struggled to put myself first, unsure of my self-identity, uncomfortable with self-care, and completely clueless about boundaries.

I don't resent or regret the childhood I experienced, although there were definitely times that I felt hard done by, like all children do at one point or another, especially when comparing myself to my peers. As a self-aware, conscious adult I now recognise the importance of who I was born to be, the ups and downs I experienced along the way, and all of the lessons I learnt to mould me into this person I've become.

I was given strong foundations to build upon, and I'm so grateful for that. Every pivotal moment, no matter how chaotic or dramatic it got, pushed me onwards and upwards to this new and improved life, consistently abundant and consistently upgrading.

While I view much of what I experienced as meant to be, I also had control over how quickly, smoothly, and consciously I travelled from one milestone to the next. It was, and still is, a bittersweet collaboration of free will and destiny. I always had the ability to manifest my circumstances, and I unknowingly did, but I also couldn't avoid the lessons I needed to learn to become the me I was meant to be, and the knowledge and experience to do what I was meant to do.

We all manifest what we experience, but we're usually oblivious to the part we play in the construct of our seemingly random lives, unaware that even the bad times serve our highest good. Everything we are, and have, right now is the result of our own previous thoughts and feelings, meandering towards the end goal of what we were brought here to do. By taking ownership of the reality we create for ourselves, we can consciously analyse why something happened, learn from it, and deliberately create new possibilities for ourselves.

I've seen the Law of Attraction at work in my life, whether I've deliberately made something happen or triggered it by accident. I've watched the process evolve with awe, often in a state of disbelief, as my thoughts became things. When I realised that we all have this superpower at our fingertips, I couldn't shut up about it, and that just made it show up in my life even more. The thing to bear in mind, though, is that it's not a tool to use with greed, or gluttony. It's just one skill in the toolkit of living a mindful, self-aware life that enables us to move towards what we want.

Living with this awareness of the Law of Attraction has been a magical experience. I've been lucky enough to witness the manifestation of homes and cars, even relationships I wanted, seemingly turn up out of the blue but, when I look back I can see I did put in the work and these miracles didn't appear out of thin air overnight.

Being a conscious observer of this process is fascinating. It's like living in a fantasy world of your own making, where you've tapped into this secret magic power. It seems too good to be true. It seems like you're dreaming, but you're not. I want to pinch myself every day, and the truly crazy part is that everyone's using the Law of Attraction; they just don't know it yet.

There's an abundance of real life stories, and case studies, of the Law of Attraction in action. You might have come across them, or you might want to put the book down and have a little Google now, because instead of repeating those same stories for you, I'm going to tell you a few of my own.

MANIFESTING HOUSES

When I moved back to Bournemouth to support my mum through some hard times, I gave up the live-in job I had in Cambridge to find my mum somewhere to live, which meant moving in as well, just for the time being, into a small one bedroom flat. It was cramped and living with my mum again, after decades of not, felt strange. I love my own company and my own space. I'm the kind of person who needs a sanctuary; somewhere I can retreat to and be alone.

I was working part-time in an office, not earning very much, as a stop-gap. I knew I couldn't afford my own place, and I wasn't sure what I was going to do beyond making sure my mum was okay. That was my priority, and I told myself everything else could wait... but my daydreams naturally drifted towards having a place of my own, light, airy, maybe with a little green space, peaceful, quiet, and just big enough for me to get away from the world when I needed to. As I regularly took myself away to this imagined place, and enjoyed the peaceful happiness it gave me as if I was really there, I unknowingly triggered the Law of Attraction.

Although I had set mum up with a flat, someone I worked with knew what I had been trying to do, and mentioned that a place had become vacant that might be even more perfect for my mum. I agreed to a viewing and booked an appointment, but when I told her about it she wasn't interested. She said she was happy where she was. Being polite I attended the viewing anyway, intending to turn it down with some made up excuse, but when I walked through the front door I was struck by the overwhelming realisation that this little house was actually meant for me.

It was light, airy, and just big enough for one. It even had a little courtyard garden, filled with green plants, and my intuition screamed at me that this was the Law of Attraction delivering exactly what I wanted. I said yes to the house, despite knowing I couldn't afford it. I knew that somehow I would make it happen, that the universe would provide, just like it put this house in front of me. I just knew in my gut that it was meant to be.

At work the next day, I stressed over my low income, even though I knew I shouldn't doubt this possibility. I wondered how I would afford this house by myself. I wanted it and I believed in it, as a gift from the universe answering my own calling out for it, but how could I sign a tenancy agreement knowing what I earned wouldn't be enough?

Maintaining my belief in the goodwill of the universe, I asked for a sign. I thought to myself, and to the ether, that if the Law of Attraction was at work here, if I was really supposed to believe that the universe had delivered, surely I could ask for a clear definitive sign and get one; a sign that I could actually have what I wanted, that I could somehow afford to live there. So I asked, and then got busy with work, shaking the doubts from my mind.

Within an hour I was head-hunted, through a friendly Facebook message, for a local working role that would put all of my creative and practical experience, and knowledge, into practice. It was pretty much the perfect fit for me, despite the fact I hadn't even put the feelers out to find a new job yet. It landed in my lap out of nowhere.

Then I got a phone call to write a huge amount of material for a previous client I hadn't worked for in months, with a quick turnaround deadline, to be paid by the end of the week. Within an hour of asking for a sign, while simultaneously trusting that if I was meant to have this house I would, I was suddenly able to afford it.

So everything fell into place, I moved into that little house for one, and loved every day I spent there. I had a sanctuary again, the light airy peace and quiet I thrive on, a little green space, and my own place to call home. My belief in the Law of Attraction was reaffirmed.

When it came to leaving that little house, to move to the big city lights of London, and upgrade my life once again, I was so grateful for the time I spent there, not attached to the material substance of it, or to the comfort zone I had begun to dwell in.

I said goodbye with love, appreciation, and excitement for the next steps I was going to take, but I've never forgotten the mysterious way everything fell into place for me to live there, and the indisputable proof that the Law of Attraction really is at work in my life.

MANIFESTING CARS

After manifesting my little house, my little sanctuary, and my belief in the Law of Attraction had grown stronger than ever, I continued to see its magic working on me. The next thing I manifested was my ultimate dream car.

The classic Audi TT had been my dream car since before I learnt to drive. Over the years I worked my way up from a little black Ford KA to the convertible version, the Ford Street KA, and loved driving them both. Any other car didn't really cross my mind, I was utterly in love with each car and grateful for what I had at the time.

When my beloved Street KA failed its MOT, and the cost of repairs was more than the car was worth, I knew it was time to say goodbye. I was genuinely upset to have to let it go, and resented having to walk and get the train to work, turning a 15 minute journey into an hour commute twice a day. It was a pain to get around without a car, having become so used to nipping here, there and everywhere at a moment's notice.

I was begrudgingly making that daily journey, cursing the wrong shoes one day and the train delays the next, but knowing what I know about optimistic thinking, and trying to see every negative experience as a positive or a lesson, I decided to have a word with myself.

I briefly wondered if the universe was making space in my life for an upgrade, and imagined driving my very own Audi TT to work, roof down, wind whipping through my hair in the sunshine. I entertained the dialogue between me and the ether, surrendered the thought to the universe, and trusted it to show up in my life whenever it was meant to, when I was ready, when I believed I deserved it, however long it would take.

Much to my surprise, the powers that be conspired to deliver what I wanted quicker than I thought possible. I was driving an Audi TT within a week, roof down, wind whipping through my hair, the warmth of the sunshine on my face. That scenario I had experienced in my imagination had become a real life experience, once again.

I love driving and I really loved driving that car, but when I moved to London I used it less and less as I adventured across the city on the tube and train. I had to detach from a material possession yet again, but knowing how easily I had manifested that beautiful little car, I consoled myself with the belief that I could have another one in the future.

Moving to London, practically overnight, was a huge leap forwards for me and making changes was inevitable.

So I chose to say goodbye to my dream car, and made space in my life for new dreams to come in by committing to city life.

It was a relief to let go of the financial responsibility that came with maintaining, insuring and taxing a car, not to mention the parking tickets I racked up in London. I was grateful for the fun and freedom that car brought me when I needed it, but fun and freedom looked different to me in the city.

I was sad to see that car go, of course, I had been dreaming about it since I was a teenager, but I'm so grateful for what it still represents to me today. I actually manifested that car into my life, without a shadow of a doubt.

MANIFESTING MY LOVE LIFE

People don't believe it's possible, but I've actually set out to manifest a hot guy, once or twice, and succeeded. After years of absorbing material on the subject, I had an 'aha' moment and finally got my head around my Law of Attraction process. I wanted to test it step by step, so I playfully went through the process, focusing more on how I wanted to feel than what he should be like.

I then opened myself up to the different ways I could meet someone. I knew I had to detach from how it would happen, and let it be however it wanted to be. I was having no luck on dating apps, but I matched with someone new and the next day I agreed to go on a date with him.

I genuinely didn't think this was the guy I had asked for, based on his photos and conversation, but I felt like going on a single date with someone friendly and fun, with no expectation of it being more than a fun evening; just some flirty conversation over a couple of drinks in a city where I didn't know many people.

When we met I realised he was exactly what I had been trying to manifest. We hit it off instantly, he ticked all of the boxes I wanted, and for the next few months I felt how I had imagined myself feeling; relaxed, adored, able to talk openly and freely with him, sharing whatever thought popped in my head, and totally comfortable being myself.

I immersed myself in the enjoyment of this manifestation, just received what it was, amazed by what I had actually managed to attract by setting my mind to it, but I knew it was just a test pilot of the process, I knew I had some tweaks to make, I knew he wasn't the ultimate romantic lead in the movie of my life, and that took the pressure off. I allowed myself to see how I could be treated differently to how I had been treated before. It was a tiny upgrade and a big lesson.

I still had work to do on myself, mostly around my belief in what I deserved, but I was grateful for his presence in my life and the joy it brought me at that time. When the timing was right we met, when we both needed some companionship, some kind of social life, in a city that was new to us. We brought each other what we needed, taught each other lessons, and when the timing was right again we went our separate ways. It felt so easy, so relaxed, and not the struggle I was used to.

As I learnt more about the Law of Attraction, and about myself, I kept upgrading my beliefs, I faced my fears, I raised my self-worth, and I did a hell of a lot of work on my self-development. I finally spent a long time single and learning how to be happy alone, instead of being half a person, half a couple.

Eventually I reached the point where I was able to attract the absolutely perfect guy for me, and it felt like the universe hit me over the head with a frying pan. I realised this was what a healthy loving relationship was supposed to feel like, that this was what I had stopped myself from having all of my life.

I had spent my whole life believing I wanted, and deserved, a particular emotionally unavailable 'type' and that was what I got, over and over and over, including a lengthy twin flame experience that completely changed my life.

By being single and working on myself, I smashed through those lesser beliefs, realised I deserved more than I had been willing to settle for, and as if by magic I stepped into a relationship that still feels like a dream. I want to pinch myself every day, and I still ask him where he came from.

This relationship, and this man of my dreams, feels like a gift from the universe. Our consistently blossoming life together feels like a reward for all of the hard work I put in over years of struggle and learning, to get to where I am today, and I am so grateful for all of the hardships, the failed relationships, and the lessons I learnt from them. I don't regret a moment, or the pace at which I evolved, because it all led me to here.

MANIFESTING LESSONS

I've witnessed so many unconscious manifestations, lots of my own of course, but also of the people around me who complain about their circumstances, wishing they were free of them, only to miss those things when they get taken away.

It reminds me that I should be careful what I wish for, that I should lean away from negativity as much as possible, but I also trust the universe to act in favour of my highest good. Even the bad stuff serves a purpose. I learn from the bad times, I evolve through my hardships, and I grow out of the darkness up towards the light. Like the Buddhist saying goes - no mud, no lotus.

Once I became aware of this process, aware that it's in action all the time, responding to my thoughts, my desires, and even my fears, I began to accept that I'm responsible for everything occurring in my life. The good, the bad, and the ugly, have manifested because of me, whether I wanted it to or not. The negative experiences are just stepping stones towards an upgrade, like downloading new software to prepare me for the next level, and when I lose something, or can't have something I think I want, it creates space in my life for something better. So there's never any need to freak out.

Learning that I had the power to work with the Law of Attraction, just like everyone else, didn't cause a huge disaster in my life; nothing changed in that moment. Simply knowing about the Law of Attraction didn't mean my life was any different to when I didn't know that was the case. Life had been travelling along on its own course regardless of knowing how I affected it. The difference now is that I have the knowledge and awareness to take control of how I behave within the universe, and how it responds to me. I know how to change my perception of what happens, be conscious of how much work I put in to play my part in the process, and how to keep moving, up through the upgrades ahead of me.

It took me years to get my head around this stuff, but I got there in the end, and now I want to pass on my knowledge, my understanding, my point of view on the Law of Attraction, by explaining how you can work with it to upgrade your life too.

So take a breath, get comfy, and relax. Don't freak out. It will take some time, but you'll get there.

Chapter Two

THE LAW OF ATTRACTION

This is not Amazon Prime. Don't expect to request a pony, or a yacht, or the man of your dreams, and see it turn up on your doorstep the next day.

WHAT THE LAW OF ATTRACTION IS NOT

SOME PEOPLE THINK that when they start applying the Law of Attraction to their lives, they can magically manifest everything they want with a click of their fingers, as if Aladdin's genie will turn up to grant their wishes, or Cinderella's fairy godmother will come along and swish her wand. When they find out they don't actually live in a Disney movie they give up.

Amazon Prime has become our real life version of the genie. Whatever trivial 'stuff' you want can and will appear on your doorstep the next day. It comes at a price, which okay, you've worked for that money and you can spend it how you like, but what about the stuff you can't afford or can't buy? What about love, money and success? You can't buy those on Amazon.

WHAT IS THE LAW OF ATTRACTION?

The Law of Attraction is recognised as a popular set of instructions that people everywhere are using to manifest the life of their dreams. It has become a system we can all apply to turn our imagined thoughts, ideas, dreams and wishes into real life things, successes, and experiences.

If you're reading this book, you've probably already heard of the Law of Attraction. Perhaps you already have a vague idea of what it is; perhaps you've read other books, and tried to learn about it from other resources, and perhaps, you're confused and frustrated by all the information, like I was.

You're keen to know how you can make it work for you, how you can manifest whatever you want in your life, how to make all your wildest dreams come true. You may have read all the books, watched all the videos, taken all the courses, like I did, and still feel lost. So I want to fill in the gaps, I want to help you help yourself, by sharing my knowledge and understanding of how it works, and how to make it work for you. This is my understanding of the Law of Attraction.

The Law of Attraction is not a magic trick. Nor is it something you need to switch on. It's a law of nature, woven into the fabric of the universe. It's the fundamental behind-the-scenes process generating everything we experience in our lives.

It causes you to drive straight into a parking spot at the supermarket, it causes you to pick the last of your favourite chocolate bars from the shelf, it causes you to easily find your keys when you lose them, it causes you to get that place on the university course you wanted, it even causes you to pick the winning lottery numbers.

The Law of Attraction governs our entire reality, it generates the stuff of life, it keeps things rolling in the direction we expect them to roll, and it occasionally causes miracles.

You don't have to know anything about the Law of Attraction to make it work for you, it already does. It's working overtime, day and night; to put together every little thing you experience, good and bad, from birth to death. It's working for all of us, all the time, like a programme running in the background maintaining the reality we expect to see.

YOU'RE THE CAUSE

People who have never heard of the Law of Attraction are still affected by it; their lives, as well as yours and mine, are entirely based on this law. The grades you got in school, the career path you've taken, the relationships you've gone through, and perhaps are still in, are the result of your collaboration with the Law of Attraction.

Everything in your life, every moment, every experience, every material thing you have come to own, has been created by you, as you've unknowingly been working with the Law of Attraction.

Every choice you make, every reaction you have, everything you are, do, and think is a part of this process. It reacts to you, your beliefs, your emotions, even your thoughts, making you 100% responsible for everything in your life, with no exception.

I know that might be a hard pill to swallow, it might be hard to believe, but it's true. We have been oblivious to this law most of our lives, and yet, it has been working on our behalf this whole time, reacting to us and our vibrational frequencies.

This is when some people freak out, and throw the book across the room.

You might be thinking back to all the hardships you suffered, all the bad days you went through, all the ups and downs that no one would ever ask for. You might be shouting 'how dare you accuse me of wanting xyz in my life, this is a load of bull'.

YOU ALWAYS HAVE A CHOICE

The Law of Attraction is not a person, it's a process. It doesn't have the capacity for sympathy or empathy. It just does its job, and it does it to perfection, every time. Whatever you focus your attention on, it says yes to.

If you're thinking I'm amazing, I'm so talented, I'm contributing great things to this world and I deserve to be well-paid for it, you'll get a resounding yes, and you'll start to see the hard evidence that supports your vibrational frequency.

If you think I'm broke, I'm a loser, and I'm not good enough for the guy or girl I've got my eye on, you'll get a resounding yes, and you'll start to see the hard evidence that supports your vibrational frequency. Get it?

If you accept responsibility, if you take ownership of your life, if you step up to become aware of your thoughts, feelings and beliefs, and if you change them to match the reality you want to experience instead of what has passed, you'll get a resounding yes.

You are more than capable of steering the Law of Attraction in the direction you want to go in. You are not less deserving than anyone else. There is no difference between you and whoever you admire. You make the choices, and the Law of Attraction responds.

It's not a theory, or a concept. It's quantum physics.

GET DECISIVE

If the Law of Attraction did work like Amazon Prime, our lives would be a mess. We would all have piles of packages landing on our doorsteps in such a continual influx that we wouldn't be able to move.

As you look around at the infinite possibilities of what you could have, you would be instantly ordering everything you liked just by thinking about it. One second you want a yacht, then a pony, then a hunky blonde fireman, then a dark brooding bad boy, then a puppy, then a pizza, then the world's largest banana pancake. The madness would never end.

Like a kid with too many Christmas presents, you won't know what to play with first, you'll be bored before you know it, you'll get nothing done and, besides, where are you going to store all of these deliveries?

Eventually you'd expect to get an error message saying,

'Make up your bloody mind, already.'

You have to be more decisive than that. The Law of Attraction doesn't respond to our every whim, it supports us with the desires we truly focus on, the things we're willing to put our all into getting. It's a 50/50 deal. You have to do the work you're guided to do, and the Law of Attraction will match your effort. So if you're not prepared to be a team player in this, you simply don't want it badly enough.

HOW DOES IT MAKE YOU FEEL?

The world we live in today has made a lot of us a little too fixated on material possessions. We're fed very effective advertising that makes people want the latest model of something they already have, they want bigger and better, or smaller and sleeker, they want what everyone else seems to have, and they're continually taught that they need more and more money in order to keep up with the stuff they're convinced they should be buying.

What you want is your prerogative. There's no judgement here. Money is not evil, and wanting to live the best life you can imagine, wanting a more luxurious lifestyle, being able to travel and have that freedom you dream about having is absolutely fine, but what you want, is not actually the thing itself, it's how it makes you feel. All of these material things are connected to a feeling. Having this, or that, will make you feel a certain way, and THAT is what you're actually seeking, that feeling. Think about it.

More money might make you feel free to spend it however you want, and that house might make you feel more secure, stable or successful. It's a feeling you seek, not the thing, and that's what the Law of Attraction responds to – the vibrational frequency of your feeling, you want the hard evidence that supports you living in that state.

The simplest way to make the Law of Attraction work in your favour, in a non-specific sense, is to simply feel good as often as you can. By thinking positive thoughts, by turning anything you experience into an upgrade towards benefiting your life, by choosing to believe that you are always moving upwards towards the best version of yourself and any hardships you go through are lessons acting in your best interests, by choosing to turn away from any negativity you face, and consistently making yourself feel joy on a daily basis, you will attract more positive experiences into your life.

It doesn't have to take tons of work once you get the hang of it, it doesn't have to be a long hard slog, it can be as simple as filling yourself with that natural high feeling in any moment.

You really are capable of pausing whatever you're feeling and switching it up. You can make yourself, or allow yourself, to feel whichever feeling you choose. This can take a bit of practice, but it is doable.

Concentrate your attention on a feeling. Imagine feeling the happiest you can possibly feel, and flood your body with that feeling. That's it. Do that as often as you can, do it while walking, or driving, or cleaning, or washing. Simply listening to some upbeat music, meditating, journaling, getting some exercise, or doing a quick yoga practice are great shortcuts towards raising your mood.

This is how the Law of Attraction works at its most basic level. However you feel, repeatedly and consistently, is what triggers the attraction process; it makes you attractive to more experiences that make you feel the same way.

Just being aware of how you're feeling is a key step to steering the Law of Attraction in the direction you want to go.

HOW MUCH DO YOU DESERVE?

No matter what it is you want you can have it. You just have to believe you can have it, that you're worthy of it, that you deserve it.

Whatever you believe to be real, and possible for you, comes to be so. This is paramount in understanding the

Law of Attraction. It is your belief system that creates the restrictions. If you believe you will only ever achieve so much, then that is how much you will achieve. If you believe you can only reach a certain level of success, or that you're only good enough to reach a certain level in life and love, then that will be the reality you experience.

So in applying the Law of Attraction to your life, you actually have some groundwork to do on yourself. You have to truly believe you deserve the reality you want to manifest. You have to truly believe you are good enough to attract it. You have to truly believe it's possible for you. It doesn't matter where anyone starts in life; everyone has the capacity to make the Law of Attraction work for them.

There's also this strange belief that there's only so much to go around, that there's only so much money, or success, or even love for some of the global population to experience. People believe there's some kind of system in place that keeps some people down and raises some people up. This is utter nonsense. There is no limit on abundance, there is no limit on possibilities, and there's no limit on the number of directions your life can go in. Plus, YOU are in charge of your life and your experience, no one else.

If someone else can have it, so can you. If you begin to see the people around you with that thing you want, there's no need to be jealous. If you can see it in existence, if it's popping up in your daily life, practically taunting you, that just means it's getting closer to becoming a part of your own life too.

If you believe you deserve it, you do, and that in itself unblocks you from having it. Accepting that you can have anything and everything opens up the path for you to walk forwards and have it all.

STOP BELIEVING, START KNOWING

One of the challenges nearly all people face when trying to learn and apply this stuff is their level of belief. They consistently try to believe that they'll see their manifestations come to life, and it's this believing in manifesting that actually holds them back.

Believing in something is not the same as knowing something's true. Manifesting things makes this process sound like a magic trick, as if there'll be a purple cloud of smoke and what you want will magically appear. No.

Knowing that what you want is already out there, that it exists, even if it's not yet in your hands, is enough to set you on the path to finding it. You're not manifesting something out of thin air. What you want already exists. You're going to follow your intuition to find it, claim it, and make it yours.

Knowing something is a much stronger vibrational frequency than believing something. There's no room for doubt, there's no room for opinion, and there's no room for questioning the possibility of something when you've already accepted it as a fact.

THE LAW OF ATTRACTION WORKS WITH YOU NOT FOR YOU

You can have everything you want. You just have to be prepared to do a little work, to play your part, to work

23

WITH the Law of Attraction, and actually move forwards towards your dreams, in order to make them happen. The universe isn't going to ring your doorbell and say,

'Good morning, madam, here's the life upgrade you ordered.'

It's in our nature to want to work for something, to want to be challenged, to learn and grow, and move in the direction of our goals, satisfied that we deserve what we want when we get it.

That's what makes life exciting, that's what makes life worthwhile. As we acquire knowledge and experience over time, as we learn, grow, and evolve into better versions of ourselves, we learn bits and bobs that help us along the way, like what's right and what's wrong, how our minds work, what's good and bad for us, which mistakes not to make again and again, and how to work with the Law of Attraction.

YOU'RE READY

The fact that you're reading this book right now means you're ready. You're ready to consider the Law of Attraction as a real thing, and how it affects your life. You'll start to notice how it has affected you all along, how people, occasions, interactions, incidents lined up to get you to where you are today. You'll realise that coincidences weren't coincides at all, you were simply moving into alignment with getting what you wanted, or what you persistently focused on. Good and bad.

Now that you're aware of the Law of Attraction, you can't be made unaware. When you're ready to take the steps needed to steer your life in the direction you want it to go, you will, and you'll see incredible results if you stick with it.

Chapter Three

THE HUMAN SUPERPOWER

Step into the best version of you today.

YOU HAVE POWER

YOUR IMAGINATION IS the strongest power you have. You can imagine anything. You can picture your life completely differently to how it is. You can choose to see whatever it is you want to see. You always have a choice, you always have options.

You can choose to let something drag you down, or lift you up. You can take the worst experiences of your life and turn them into lessons, choosing to learn from the hardships you go through, or allowing them to cause a domino effect, seeing negative repercussions, and experiencing drama and obstacles everywhere you go.

When you wake up and get out of 'the wrong side of the bed', perhaps stubbing your toe, then spilling coffee down your clean white outfit, making you late, and you miss the bus, this is because negative thinking and negative reactions attract more of the same. You could choose to stop and laugh it off instead. You could choose to switch into a positive mind-set and prevent a bad morning becoming a bad day.

POSITIVITY POWER

The power of positive thinking has even been proven to affect your physical health; people have overcome serious illnesses by researching and applying focused positive thought. Seriously, scientific studies have been conducted, reported, and changed the way people think about their health.

You can benefit too. You can choose to be more positive right now, and you can apply it to anything. Your thoughts, your imagination, are so powerful. Why wouldn't you choose to use them for your own benefit?

Your beliefs of what is possible, what you're capable of, and what you deserve to experience in life are paramount. Any limitations you believe in are the only restrictions you face. They're self-imposed.

Any blocks, barriers, and limitations you've unknowingly put on yourself, anything you've put in place to hold yourself back can be changed at any time. Use the power of your imagination, deliberately lean towards a more positive mind-set and your whole life will change.

THINK LIKE A CHILD

As a child, you happily used your imagination openly, freely, playfully, and created fantasy scenarios that satisfied every wish. Nothing held you back. You made all your dreams come true through the power of your imagination. You explored any idea that piqued your curiosity, and you role-played future possibilities with reckless abandon. You didn't give any thought to limitations, restrictions, blocks or barriers. You believed you could be, have and do anything, and you were right.

As a child, you weren't yet conditioned by any outside comments, comparisons with others, or imposed beliefs that stopped you from the life you wanted to live, you didn't wonder how you would do something, you believed wholeheartedly that the future was yours, and the life ahead of you was of your own making. When did that change?

As you grew up, you took on external beliefs, learnt from repeated lessons, and watched your role models and peers, putting together all of these sources of information to create your store of beliefs, limitations, and understanding of how the world works. Over time, blocks and barriers against your dreams began to pile up, you accepted these blocks as fact, and you began to believe you were no longer able to have, be, or do whatever you wanted.

You used your imagination less and less, relying on evidence that the reality you saw around you was all there was, that the infinite possibilities you once entertained had become limited. You questioned your ability to create the life you really wanted. You questioned your talents, your intelligence, and your achievements in comparison to everyone else. You put yourself in a box of your own making. You made the decision to accept what others said as fact, you took on their labels as your own, defining yourself as a specific kind of person; telling yourself this is who I am, this is how much I can achieve, this is the life I deserve to live, and this is as far as I can go. You made a list of factors that had to be considered before you could move forward, before you could reach the next level of your life. You denied yourself the upgrade, and put conditions on your own ability to grow.

These beliefs and limitations are different for everyone, dependent on their individual experiences of role-models, peers, and external input. This is why some flourish quicker than others, why some people seem to achieve a lot based on confidence rather than talent, why some hold themselves back even though they're greatly talented. We're all playing in a playground of our own making.

What happened to your imagination? What happened to your curiosity? What happened to the playful nature that tested your imagination, your boundaries, your reality, your surroundings and circumstances? What happened to infinite possibility?

It's mostly the result of social conditioning, of what we're taught to believe, of how the world works, of the systems and societies we're expected to buy into, of conforming to what everyone else is doing, of seeing what others are capable of and grading ourselves on a scale that includes everyone else. We're strongly influenced by the people we come in contact with, including the heroes we look up to on social media, and it's interesting to consider the difference between East and West, of how children grow up around the world in different cultures, with different backgrounds and upbringings.

Until we come into contact with our peers, with the rest of the world, with external opinions, we still believe we're capable of anything. Born alone, and left alone, we have the power to have, be, and do anything we set our mind to. Of course, we also need external input to learn, grow, and become human beings interacting with civilisation, but it is only with the rules and restrictions we take on that our imagination dwindles and becomes limited.

Your imagination sets you apart from animals, your conscious thinking and self-awareness provides you with infinite possibilities. Your individual perspective on absolutely anything can change your life experience in a second. You can flip any negative into a positive, simply by choosing to think about it differently. You don't have to be dampened by the dark clouds of a rainy day, you can choose to be grateful for the rain that waters the flowers, that prevents this country from experiencing drought, that nourishes the food you eat and the abundant life you enjoy.

You can choose to switch your perspective and experience an entirely different reality, if you want to, causing you to feel as high as you want to feel, in any moment. This ability is like a superpower, it's your very own source of magic and miracles. Your reality is what you perceive it to be, you can interpret it however you choose. Nothing has to be what you are told it is, or previously believed it to be. Have you ever considered how incredible that is?

Visualising the life you want to live can take you in the direction of making it your reality. Using your imagination to transport you into a different life, making a quantum leap into another timeline, with no holds barred, opens up the doorway to actually being there. By entertaining anything your mind wants to show you, without limiting yourself by questioning the journey of how you can get there, allows you access to a destination you previously thought impossible. You can upgrade your life little by little, from what it looks like today, to the distant future you dream of living in. You can move up from home to home, switch careers, meet the person of your dreams, drive that car you think you can't afford, and nourish the kind of lifestyle you want and deserve to have. Don't

Kerry Laws

worry about the route you'll take, or the obstacles and challenges you might face on the way, the universe will be your guide, and provide the resources you need to make it happen.

Begin by exercising your imagination. Play with it. Stretch it as far as you can. Go wild with options, and delve deep into your dreams. Until you wander into the imagined realities of every kind of life you might want to live, you won't know what you truly want, and you can't have what you want until you know what it is, what it looks like, and most importantly what it feels like, specifically to you.

You have the superpower to experience any kind of life you want through your imagination. Do you like the look of a celebrity's life, a neighbour's, a friend's, or the luxurious lifestyle of your rich uncle and his family? If you think it looks good from the outside, try it out from the inside, using your imagination. Then decide if that's really what you want, if there's something you would tweak, change, add or delete, to make it your own. Maybe you wouldn't want to work as much as your uncle to make all that money, leaving you with no free time to enjoy it, so you want a career that allows you to work from home or remotely, or not work at all. Maybe there's a different version of what you originally thought you wanted that you would prefer. You won't know until you try it.

Use your imagination to find clarity. Work out what you truly want, and keep imagining it, as a regular practice, until you know for sure that this is what you want to attract into your life. If something else catches your eye, switch it up. It's your imagination, no one else's. What you want to use it for is entirely up to you.

INNER CHILD WORK

Many of us have lost touch with our imaginative abilities, hardened by the slog of adulthood. Reconnecting with your imagination might require reconnecting with your inner child, perhaps even re-parenting that part of yourself, and letting your inner child come out to play.

It doesn't have to mean playing like you did as a child, although that's often the most direct way to do it, it can simply be a case of finding out what you like to do for fun, what makes you feel that pure sense of joy. Some people refer to it as being in the zone, or in flow, and it often happens when you're working on something you're passionate about, when you're so fully immersed in an activity you love that nothing else distracts you, nothing else matters, and you eventually look at the clock surprised by how much time passed, while you got lost in whatever you were doing.

It's different for everyone, just like it was different for us as children. Some like to lose themselves in the fantasy world of a book, some get the same pleasure from role-playing video games, some like the competitive adrenalin rush of team sports, rollercoasters, running, playing on the swings, painting, drawing, writing, singing, jamming, dancing to music or getting creative with some kind of arts and crafts. It doesn't matter what it is, just that it invokes pure joy in you.

It's not always as simple as it sounds. Some people really struggle with reconnecting with that part of their inner self, with allowing themselves to play and have fun without feeling guilty about what they think they 'should' be doing, but there are lots of coaches, courses, and interactive workshops that can guide the work you need to do to encourage the childlike curiosity to come back to the surface. You don't have to do it alone, and you don't have to feel lost in this process.

I spent four days on a spiritually focused, self-development retreat where my inner child was invited to come to the surface. I was tasked with writing a letter to my inner child and I sobbed as I told her she didn't have to be the grown up anymore, she could be the child she always wanted to be and enjoy the childhood fun she always felt she missed out on. After consoling and comforting that part of myself, telling her I would take care of the grown up stuff now, while she could play without a care in the world, she went straight for a tyre swing on the grounds, giggling and swinging, running around being silly, and laughing with the new friends she had made in the silence of the retreat.

By making peace with that part of me, by re-parenting my inner child, by allowing her to have fun and see the less serious side of life, I became lighter, curious, wide-eyed and open-hearted, exploring the world with childlike wonder, inspiring new creative paths, and travelling along with a skip in my step. I live alongside my inner child now, allowing her to appreciate the wonder of the world around us whenever it catches her eye.

I now notice people living with their own inner children at the surface. I saw a young woman in her twenties, with her earphones in, singing aloud on the tube... She was singing 'part of your world' from the little mermaid with a big smile on her face not caring that people were staring, although a few people smiled and hummed along. So many people find a way to balance their day with a little fun, something that makes them smile, and nourishes that forever young part of them.

What did you like to do as a child; did you climb trees, play games, draw, paint, sing, or dance around in your room? If you listen carefully you'll hear your inner child's cries for attention, and find out what would satisfy their need to be held, by you. Hold space for that part of you, and consider how you could become friends with your inner child. Allow yourself to nourish your childlike curiosity, your wonder, and your imagination as an adult.

Chapter Four

THE SCIENCE

*The universe says yes. Good or bad. Whatever
you think, whatever you feel, whatever
you believe. The universe says yes.*

LAWS OF NATURE

OUR LIVES ARE governed by many laws of nature, such as gravity, the law of cause and effect, the speed of light, the law of attraction, and many others. These laws are not biased towards some people and not others, they are not magic tricks or illusions, and they are not switched on by your attention. These laws of nature exist with or without your knowledge of them.

Gravity doesn't stop working because you stop thinking about it, you don't see a random child floating off into the sky like a human shaped balloon just because she hasn't heard of gravity. Gravity is a universal law that cannot be denied or refuted, a fixed condition of the universe, which existed long before Isaac Newton proved it to the world.

Gravity has always been there, an essential part of the universe that keeps everything in order, running with precision, and orbiting like it should. Gravity exists regardless of whether it gets any recognition, working day and night, from the dawn till the end of time, and the same goes for the Law of Attraction.

Once science points them out, these laws of nature become concepts we accept as fact. We learn how they affect our entire existence and experience of life, and that they always did, we just didn't know. We become aware of these laws through scientific theory, proven by extensive practical experimentation and studies, backed up by statistics, but there is no arguing that they exist with or without our acknowledgment of them.

The Law of Attraction is just one of these laws of nature that govern our universe. The Law of Attraction exists with or without you, it does its thing whether you pay attention to it or not, working behind the scenes all the time, just like the other laws.

We take advantage of these laws all the time, whether we know it or not. Our world, our lives, and the entire universe would be very different without them. We need gravity to literally keep our feet on the ground, the roots of trees in the earth, the planets in orbit, and the sun where it is, and we need the Law of Attraction to govern the flow of like attracting like, responding to us, and creating our individual experiences, so we don't all repeat the same human life.

We are all unique. We are each made up of a unique combination of ingredients to become completely one-of-a-kind human beings. We come with unique backgrounds, upbringings, childhood issues, traumas, psychological make-up, social influences, educational and cultural expectations, countries of origin, and individual choices in dreams, desires and priorities.

All of that dictates who we each become, significantly different to everyone else. Each unique person has their own unique perspective on life, focused on their own particular pleasure and pain points. This directs our individual wants and needs and we communicate these with the universe, mostly oblivious to our power and the responsibility we have for our own circumstances. It is the Law of Attraction that creates our life experience in response to whatever we keep putting out into the universe.

WHAT IS THE UNIVERSE?

When we talk about the universe we often think of it as separate from us, we picture the starry night sky, the expanse of space still unexplored, distant planets, galaxies, and black-holes, we see in sci-fi movies. We think of the REST of the universe outside our planet, but actually the universe refers to everything, including Earth, and us.

We ARE the universe, and our existence within this incredible mindboggling infrastructure is essential to any of this existing at all. There is no separation when you truly break it down, because everything is made of the same stuff at its most basic level.

The entire universe is made of energy. We, and everything we can see, touch, feel, hear, taste, and all the things we can't, break down into miniscule atoms of energy. These teeny tiny atoms vibrate at different frequencies, and the differing frequencies dictate how they appear to us. Solids, liquids, and gases vibrate at different frequencies.

The words we speak, and the sounds we hear, are waves of vibration translated by our ear drums. You might have learnt this stuff in science class at school. If a tree falls in an empty forest, with no one around to hear it, would it make a sound? The waves of vibration would still echo out from the movement, rippling through all of the atoms in the air, but those waves of vibration would need an ear drum to translate them into sound as we know it.

You might have also learnt that the thoughts we think, and the emotions we feel, are also vibrations. These kinds of vibrations are translated and received in a different way, by us and by the universe. Some people are more sensitive to these vibrations, they have the ability to sense emotions, and read people in ways that most of us aren't open to.

The universe is conscious of all of the differing vibrations and frequencies occurring within it, like a complicated web of connected networks, firing off messages and relevant responses all the time. We are part of that mass of energy, holding our own vibrational state within this much bigger framework, interacting with the universe just by existing within it.

Our thoughts, our feelings, our intentions, and our actions all communicate outwards, rippling through the atoms of energy that make up the universe, sending out messages that state who and what each of us are, and what we want to experience in our lives.

IN DIALOGUE WITH THE UNIVERSE

So how do we communicate with the universe, and declare what we want, so that we can work with the Law of Attraction to make it happen? Get ready for the complicated bit.

We are conscious communicative beings, with opposable thumbs, likes, dislikes, and will power. We are godlike creatures capable of creation and destruction. We have so much incredible magical potential, and access to infinite possibilities. Just take a minute to really take that all in, and shake off the limitations you've built around you. Now consider the mysterious miraculous nature of your own mind and that science hasn't even discovered how much more the human mind is capable of.

Anyway, the mind is made up of three sections, the conscious, the subconscious and the unconscious. They each serve a purpose. They each process different thoughts, feelings and beliefs.

THE CONSCIOUS MIND

The conscious is the part of the mind you'll be most familiar with. It is the constant running commentary you hear during your waking hours. Conscious thought is the part of the mind we have direct and fairly easy control over. We're capable of deliberately choosing to think positively or negatively, telling ourselves how to feel, how to behave, and how to interpret what we experience in any given moment.

The conscious mind is what you're going to be working with, taming it and tweaking it, to make it work better for you. Getting your conscious mind to behave itself causes the subconscious to do the same, creating a domino effect that emits a positive frequency into the universe and tells it what you want.

Left to its own devices, your inner voice will be a relentless stream of flowing chatter, an inner commentator running on autopilot - fleeting, ever-changing, and giving unnecessary attention to the rollercoaster of emotions that rise and fall throughout the day, which might be harmless most of the time, but there are varying reasons why you need to tame this inner voice and make sure it's on your side.

THE SUBCONSCIOUS MIND

While your daily mind chatter is only really for you, over time these thoughts and feelings repeat themselves. The more you loop the same thought, and naturally seek out the hard evidence in your life to support it, the quicker it turns into a strongly held belief that this is all you're ever going to experience. So if you think you don't have enough money, you're going to keep checking your bank balance, or looking at purchases that you know are out of your price range. You've found the evidence to support that thought and turned it into the belief that you don't have enough.

You need to recognise that you're choosing to do that to yourself. You have the alternative to live within your means, to realise that you already have what you need, even if that only means your basic needs are met, and be grateful that you're able to provide for yourself. Whichever thought pattern you choose to repeat becomes a belief, and this catches the attention of your subconscious.

The subconscious part of your mind is where your beliefs, repetitive thought patterns, and memories are stored. This is also how your mind communicates with the universe, declaring what you believe is your reality, working with the Law of Attraction to find the evidence that supports what you believe to be true. You're effectively declaring that this is the life you're choosing and you want more of the same.

The subconscious part of your mind acts like a bridge between you and the universe. Think of it as a portal, a doorway, through which you unknowingly send messages in little green glass bottles to float up through the stars and out into the ether. These messages are based on your beliefs. Your beliefs about who you are, how you feel, what you deserve, what you know and the work you're willing to put in to get what you want. These messages go out into the universe on a vibrational frequency, much like tuning into a particular radio station, and you are the one turning the dial to tune it in.

The state of being has the strongest vibration, because there is no doubt that what you are is real, you are existing in this state, this feeling or emotion, so you believe it to be true. Therefore feeling something has a stronger vibration than thinking something, and your belief in how you feel is hard to question compared with a thought. You can easily argue with a thought and, depending on how nicely you talk to yourself, there's a good chance that your inner voice will talk you out of what you're trying to make yourself believe.

In order to be consistent in your thoughts, in order for the repetitions to flow through to your subconscious programming and become automatic thought patterns that interact on a vibrational frequency level with the fabric of the universe, you have to believe them to be absolutely true.

The best way to do this is to change your thought into a feeling, make yourself feel that way repeatedly, consistently, and soon it will become a state of being that you fully believe you are capable of stepping into.

The subconscious will pick up on this repetitive behaviour, adding it to the database of who you are, a state you regularly choose to live in, and the Law of Attraction will respond in kind, helping you find the evidence you need to support this belief.

So, it's with the subconscious mind that we talk to the universe. The repetitive habitual thought patterns that run on a loop through the conscious mind get upgraded to beliefs in the subconscious, which then tells the universe what we believe, how we interpret the reality we are experiencing, and what we want to see more of.

Whatever we say in our subconscious mind, the universe says yes to. If we say I am so poor, I am struggling to pay these bills, the universe says yes you are. If we say I am happy with whatever I have, I am happy with my life the way it is, the universe says yes you are and creates more experiences that make you feel the same way.

The subconscious mind is seemingly out of our control. It is not an area of the mind we have access to, unlike the conscious part. It builds its own chanting mantra based on what we continue to focus on. So how can we edit our subconscious mind to play a loop of positive messages that invite the universe to say yes to what we want, instead of the negative messages that perpetuate more of the same?

The conscious mind is filtered through the subconscious. The subconscious picks up on the repeated statements, beliefs, and persistent messages. Like intelligent advertising on the internet and social media, the subconscious mind works like an algorithm. It tracks the words, phrases, images, and emotions we consistently use, to determine our interests. It sees you replaying that memory of a difficult time and assumes you want more of the same. It translates the repetitive activity into a language of vibrations, and the universe recognises and responds in kind, thus creating the reality you see and experience around you. This is often why we experience a string of bad luck, because we're repetitively focusing on it, fixating on the negative, and the universe says yes, here's what you want, here's more of the same.

So, it's only logical that our repetitive thinking patterns and beliefs are what filter through, from the conscious mind, to the subconscious mind, to the universe. This is why affirmations and rituals are so effective. By consistently repeating something positive in our conscious thinking, eventually our subconscious picks up on it, relays it to the universe, and the universe says yes.

THE UNCONSCIOUS MIND

The unconscious mind is responsible for your dreams, amongst other things. It's the part of your mind that processes what we've experienced during our waking hours, making sense of it in a surreal nonsensical way.

Like children mimicking the lessons they learn through the games they play, as adults we role-play scenarios in our dreams in order to face our fears, understand a difficult situation, or say the tearful goodbye we so badly needed but didn't get in real life.

When I finally met the love of my life I was visited in my dreams, by each of my ex-boyfriends. Not ideal, I thought. How do you tell your boyfriend that you dreamt about your ex last night? But it was a god thing.

My unconscious was setting up these surreal scenarios with each of them to give me back the power I didn't have at the time. The tables were turned and I was given the chance to break up and say goodbye to these guys who broke my heart, who ended things with me and, like Sarah said to the Goblin King in Labyrinth, I was finally able to say,

'You have no power over me'.

It was such a relief when I woke that first morning knowing I had mentally processed what I had gone through in that relationship, learnt from it and let it go, that I actually hoped my unconscious would do the same with another ex and it did.

Therapy, counselling and mental health services are incredible for deliberately unearthing these deep-rooted issues, allowing us to bring them up to the surface and deal with them once and for all, and I have loved the processes I've gone through with the support of some of these mental health professionals but, to be supported by your own unconscious mind, to find yourself backed up in your own dreams, to be the hero of your own movie and get your very own happy ending, is pretty damn cool.

The unconscious is a beautifully weird place. It's also a potential bridge between dimensions, allowing for astral projection and lucid dreaming, but those are topics for a whole other book. Don't underestimate the power of your mind, every part of it, every thought, every interpretation of what you experience, and every vibrational frequency you put out, serves a purpose. Every mental process is acting on your behalf, but it's triggered, at the source, by you.

YOU'RE READY FOR THIS

It might sound complicated but that's the scientific bit done. The rest of this book is less tricky to get your head around. You don't really need to understand all the behind the scenes, inner workings, stuff to work with the Law of Attraction.

We learn new things and come across certain lessons when we're ready for them, so the fact you're reading this book now means you're ready, and you can handle it. So the time has obviously come for you, to take back control, and start upgrading your life.

Chapter Five

STEP 1: DECIDE IT

*Do you really know what you want
and where you want to be?*

WHAT DO YOU WANT

NOT EVERYONE KNOWS, specifically, what it is that they want.

You might have a vague idea of how you want your life to look, but you haven't really picked out the things that need to change to get you there, or what would actually make a difference. What would make all your dreams come true? What would have you living your best life? What's making you seek the help of the Law of Attraction?

Personally, I can be pretty indecisive. I sometimes feel overwhelmed by too many options and find it hard to make a decision. So when there are infinite possibilities, when anything you can imagine you can make happen, it can feel overwhelming to simply make a choice. This overwhelm can lead to not making a decision at all, to putting it off, to telling yourself you'll think about it later, or leaving it up to fate and just seeing what happens.

WAKE-UP CALL

Were you unaware that you were putting off making decisions? Were you rolling along with the momentum of life in whatever direction it carried you, oblivious to the power you have through simply deciding what you want? Well the time is now. It's time to take responsibility for the choices you make. It's time to get clear about what it is you actually want.

First of all, accept that there is no limitation on what your life could be like. You are entitled to have, do, be, and experience anything and everything you want. You are not expected to pick one thing and put everything else aside. You really can have it all. So it really comes down to prioritising your wish list. Perhaps you want to start with something small and build up to the big stuff, or maybe there's one big thing you want that's more important to you than all the little things, so you decide to start with the big thing first. It's entirely up to you.

YOUR WISH LIST

This is just the first step, there is further work involved in the process, but you have to break it down and concentrate on each step fully. For now you just need to get very clear about what it is you want. The rest of the steps, and the universe, will help you get it. Don't worry about that now, about how, where, when and why. Just focus your attention on what it is you want, on what you want the Law of Attraction to help you get.

For me, I usually start by writing a wish list. Not just a quick 'these are the three things I want right now' kind of list, a list of EVERYTHING I could possibly want without limitations, without a budget, without any obstacles or challenges, or people standing in the way.

By writing this list, I am often surprised by how little I actually want, and by my ability to adapt my life and make some of them happen now. If I want more time, I can easily get up earlier or manage my day to make more time. I can change the way I spend money to allow for the luxuries I want, I can cut back on the frivolous daily coffees or lunches, I can walk places and save money every day by making changes, and suddenly find I can afford that expensive thing I thought I couldn't afford.

I'm also surprised by the things I don't really need to add to my life to feel happier, and the things that have already shown up, or I am on the way to having. That sense of gratitude for what I already have, that I've forgotten I once wished for, puts me in a positive vibrational state to attract more of the same.

LOVE, MONEY & SUCCESS

The big things people want are usually love, money, and success, the best motivations for working with the Law of Attraction, but these are vague concepts not real things of substance you can focus on, which makes them a little trickier but very fun to achieve.

You need to clarify what each of these concepts looks like and, more importantly, feels like, specifically to you, which we'll cover in the next chapter. The feeling we each get from love, money and success isn't the same. Money, for example, makes some people feel a sense of freedom, while for others it's a sense of security and stability. For now, just decide what it is you want.

Is there a particular kind of romantic partner you want to attract – what do they look, sound, smell, and feel like? Consider if you want to feel loved, adored, cherished, part of a team...

Is there a particular numerical figure you want to see siting in your bank account? Are there material things you can picture yourself buying when you have more money? What does your more abundant lifestyle look, sound, smell, and feel like? Consider if you want to feel freedom, security, stability…

What does success really mean to you? How will you know when you've crossed that line into what you deem as successful?

The idea of success is very different for every person, it depends what your career or lifestyle is made up of. For some, success is being at the top of their game, money in the bank, marriage, children, and a family home, while for others it could be passing a test, paying off a loan, getting into that club, or even making a difference in the world, on the frontline of a natural disaster, or rebuilding villages in third world countries.

We all have different goalposts that tend to move each time we reach them, so success really can't be measured by what anyone else is doing, or what their definition of success is, and we all have our own particular kinds of life to live that play their part and make up this kaleidoscopic collective world. You really have to think about yourself here, and what success means to you. Do not judge yourself by anyone else's standards.

So what does your successful lifestyle look, sound, smell, and feel like?

THE FIVE SENSES

You probably noticed the focus on your senses in relation to what you want, I didn't mention taste but you can absolutely add that if it applies. Maybe you want champagne with strawberries, or a celebratory cake, it's your life and your wish list. Go wild.

The five senses work on a vibrational level, just like everything else. They also work in real time. Remembering how something tasted, sounded, or felt like takes you back to a moment in time as if it were happening now. Being able to activate your senses with a memory recreates that sensation now as if it were happening in the present not the past. By experiencing something now, you're putting yourself on the vibrational frequency of what you want. So play with your imagination and your senses, to make a decision about what you want. You can pretty much time travel to where you want to be, and experience it right now in the present.

JUST MAKE A DECISION

This might seem like a simple step, yet so many of us don't really know, or haven't decided with unwavering clarity, what it is that we actually want. By leaving it open to the universe to decide for you, you're not working with the law of attraction, you're taking blind shots into the darkness guided by momentary whims, reactions, and fleeting thoughts.

You'll keep sending yourself in random directions based on your switching thought patterns, taking detours, and potentially taking the longest route possible to get to where you're meant to go.

So make a decision, get clear on what it is you want and how you want to feel. It might take more work than you expect, it might take some research, some testing, some trial and error, to find out what really makes you excited, what sparks pure joy for you. It's not always the first thing you think of, when you delve under the surface and figure out what makes you, specifically you, happy.

You also have the power to change your mind at any time, but taking detours is only going to take you longer to get there, so get the ball rolling, start moving towards the life of your dreams, and decide with unwavering clarity what it is you want.

EXERCISES TO HELP YOU DECIDE IT

SUGGESTED MEDITATION

To get into a decisive state, I recommend meditating. This doesn't have to be an extreme devotional practice. You can just sit quietly for a while, wait however long it takes for the daily mind chatter to fade away, find a place of calm within yourself, and think about what it is you really truly want. Listen to your inner self, your intuition, and take note of what comes to mind out of the stillness.

You can also practice meditating in different ways, not just sitting. You can take yourself for a walk, and think about what it is you want. Walking is very effective for switching on the creative part of your mind. The first 15 minutes are likely to be spent distracted by daily thoughts, worries, concerns, and reminders of things you've forgotten, or conversations you've had. Let your mind do its thing. Don't force it. Once that's all dealt with, your mind will join you and start to wander along with your feet.

Allow yourself to daydream, but daydream with intention. Think about that thing you want, what it looks like to you, how your senses come alive, and how the thought of having it makes you feel.

You can also do this while relaxing in the bath, while swimming, while lying in bed at night or first thing in the morning – whatever works for you. Only you know when and where you reach a calm, centred place within yourself. Then give your imagination free reign. Don't let logic, rational thinking, or social conditioning hold you back.

Anything is possible in your imagination, so forget reality for a moment and let whatever it is you want be possible.

The first time you meditate might seem tricky, and unfamiliar. Your mind will try to pull you back from fantasy land, but push past that, create a parallel life you can visit and keep going there, filling in the details each time. Enjoy your daydreams. Each time you practice, it will become easier to step into this imagined state of being and it will feel more real every time you visit.

SUGGESTED JOURNALING

If you're someone who expresses themselves through writing or drawing, you have the advantage of being familiar with putting your imagination on paper and making it real. Putting your thoughts on paper takes them out of your imagination and into the real world. They become something of substance, they become real. Even if you don't lean towards creativity in this way, I would recommend trying it.

Pick one thing to begin with, something clear and simple, maybe it's a particular car, house, or spouse. Then write about this new experience in the present tense, as if you're writing a story about yourself.

'I am driving', or 'I am living in', or 'I am in a relationship with…' and write out this scenario with yourself as the leading character, like you're living in the movie of your own life. Make it as perfect, or cheesy, or theatrical, as you like. Or you can draw, paint, even make a collage of the scenario from your visual clues, recreating the scene of your ideal life as if someone has taken a photograph, or drawn a portrait of you in this parallel life.

SUGGESTED QUESTIONS

Imagine your ideal day, when everything you want has come to pass.

How do you feel when you wake up? Where are you? What does your home look like? Maybe you're on holiday, waking in a hammock somewhere? It's up to you. Cross over from here to there - where are you sitting to write in your journal during your ideal day?

Who else is there, what do they look like, what are they doing? If it's a romantic partner you can get naughty if you like, you'll boost your emotional response and make it more powerful. Do you have children, pets, friends and family around you? Do you go out somewhere luxurious, or special, are you celebrating something?

How do you spend your time, what are you doing, how do you feel at every step? Do you work, what do you do? How do you contribute to the world in this scenario, how do you interact with other people? What's the structure of this ideal day? Go through your day, step by step, noticing the simple pleasures that make it perfect for you.

Once you've gone through your ideal day from waking in the morning to going to bed at night, look back over it and think about how much of that might be possible for you now.

If your ideal life features you waking up to a simple pleasurable routine, how can you begin incorporating that routine into your life now? What can you change today to edge towards this perfect day you've imagined?

Often, a lot of what we want is already well within our reach if we tweak our own behaviour to simply be in that frame of mind and respond with joy to what we already experience. Like, if I want more time to myself in the morning, I get up early, before anyone else gets up. If I want my ideal day to start with meditation or yoga, I can easily do that now. I don't need to wait for that some day to start living that way now.

You can return to your perfect day at any time, adding new details, changing things up, tweaking and adapting the experience every time. By doing this ideal day exercise from scratch every time, you will define the experience as more and more real, empowering the vibrational frequency and pulling your current reality in its direction.

SUGGESTED GRATITUDE PRACTICE

Sometimes I take a moment to write a list of my wants and needs, including the luxury items I think I can't afford, and quickly discover that my list is a lot shorter than I thought it was. Of course, I've been working with the Law of Attraction for a while now, and I'm continuously upgrading my life, so I don't want for much, but I'm still surprised when I do a sort of dream life stock-take and realise that I hadn't even noticed some of my manifestations turning up.

The easiest way of allowing the Law of Attraction into your life is to upgrade a little at a time. If I want more time to myself, I choose to wake up earlier, and practice making that part of my daily routine. If I want to live somewhere new, I start putting the wheels in motion to make that happen. So much is within our control, yet we often feel trapped by our circumstances.

Sometimes we allow our own dissatisfaction to

overwhelm us, we believe if I had this or that I would be happier, but when it really comes down to it, there are only a few things we really want, and a few things we used to wish for and now take for granted.

All it takes is a look back at how far we've come, from wanting something years ago, to realising that we have it now. It's usually such a gradual process to get here, and our desires are ever-changing, that we don't notice when we arrive. Every time we get something we want, or achieve that goal or dream, the goalposts move, and we move on to the next thing we want, the next life upgrade, without taking a beat to appreciate what we have now.

Practicing gratitude for what you have today, who you've become, where you are and the people you are lucky to have in your life, is vital to rewarding the Law of Attraction process for doing its work in your life. It needs to be told it's doing a good job so it knows how to keep serving you. The way to communicate that is by filling yourself up with that good feeling of gratitude, by feeling genuinely thankful for having all that you have, and thereby switching yourself onto the vibrational frequency of joy. The Law of Attraction will continue to respond in kind. You'll attract more of the same high vibrational feeling, caused by your dreams coming to fruition.

Practicing gratitude is super simple. Just write a list of things your grateful to have in your life, this can be as short as three things, including loved ones, a pay cheque, the food in the fridge, the rain that watered your garden, the sunshine, the friendly smile of a neighbour, the butterfly that flew past your nose, the love and companionship of your pet, the feel of clean bed sheets, the colour of your nail polish, your favourite TV show, or the smell of an old book. It can be absolutely anything, there's no right or wrong way to do this. You're just creating a reaction within yourself, of feeling gratitude, of feeling fortunate, of feeling simple contentedness with what you're already so lucky to have.

VISION BOARDS

Vision boards are widely used by people working with the Law of Attraction. These homemade collages are a very effective way of reminding yourself of your dreams, goals, and ambitions. They serve to trigger your imagination regularly and prompt your subconscious to move in the direction of the kind of life you want. Catching sight of a vision board on display somewhere in your environment every day will help you visualise your dreams.

Creating a vision board is a creative process of actually deciding what you want, and creating a visual prompt to keep you on track towards getting it. You simply have to find pictures that represent your ideal life; like where you want to live, holiday destinations, your ideal home, examples of a more luxurious lifestyle, even the kind of partner and future family you want to have. Then you cut and stick these pictures in a collage and display it somewhere for you to catch sight of. Seeing evidence of your dreams and embracing the feeling you get kick-starts the like attracting like process.

I've been making vision boards for a long time, so I have a method that works for me, a method I know and love. I get a cheap Ikea frame, and use the back board as my canvas to stick pictures and quotes on, which I've usually ripped from magazines. Anything that makes me feel good when I see it, anything that relates to where I want to get to, anything that causes my imagination to take me into the dream reality I want to live in.

It's all about listening to your intuition, and allowing yourself to be drawn to particular images that inspire you, that evoke a positive emotion, that will catch your eye and make you smile.

Making vision boards also acts as a mindfulness practice. Actually sitting down to put together a vision board takes your full attention, and pushes you to decide what you want with visual clarity, making you decide and declare what you want.

It depends what works for you - some of us are prompted by visual input, for others it's an audio stimulus, taste, or touch. Work with your senses to find out what sits right with you, and figure out which kind of imaginative input makes you happy. Maybe you'd prefer a playlist of music that takes you into a daydream, or a video collage of beautiful holiday destinations, or a collection of sensual fabrics and textures. There are no rules.

As a writer, I like to tell a story through most of what I do. My vision boards act like the complete setting for an upgraded lifestyle, with characters and scenarios. If I can't find the pictures I want in magazines or by printing them from the internet, I'll sketch the scenarios I want to experience instead, adding colour and real images if and when I find them.

Chapter Six

STEP 2: FEEL IT

Become a vibrational magnet by feeling it now, by feeling how your dreams coming true will make you feel.

SENDING A MESSAGE

THE NEXT STEP, after deciding with clarity what it is you want, is to get a clear message through to the universe, and invite the Law of Attraction to work with you in a new way.

You've always been communicating with the universe, and it's always been responding to you, no matter how much credit you give it. You've been guided throughout your life based on this push and pull with the universe. Now you can change and redirect the messages you're sending, you can take control of your Law of Attraction process, and take responsibility for what you make happen.

You communicate what you want with your vibration. Like tuning into a radio station, your vibrational frequency needs to match the same frequency of what you want, so that like can attract like.

GOOD VIBRATIONS

If you forget the physical being that makes you human for a minute, if you think of yourself as a bundle of energy, of atoms, vibrating at a human frequency, your vibrational state is what tells the universe you exist, it's your presence in the universe. Your vibration is what tells the universe what you are, what you want, and how to respond to you.

The Law of Attraction is only one of the ways that the universe responds, and the clue is in the name. It works the same way as a magnet - like attracts like, on a vibrational energetic level. So in order to tell the universe what you want, and how to respond to you, you need to turn yourself into an energetic magnet. You need to get yourself onto the same vibrational frequency as that thing you want.

Your vibrational frequency is just a fancy scientific way of describing how you're feeling. It's your emotional state of joy, excitement, love, happiness, sadness, frustration, anger or any other strong emotion that causes your energy to vibrate on a certain frequency.

This vibration tells the universe what kind of magnet you are, and what you will inevitably attract. Of course, most of these feelings are temporary, but if you're living in one consistent feeling or keep coming back to that feeling, you will send out the signal that you're of that frequency, and attract things of the same frequency to you.

THE KEY STATE TO BE IN

So the easiest, simplest way to make the Law of Attraction respond to you positively is to get into a consistently positive vibrational state, which just means feeling happy, and joyful, and excited as much as you can, as often as you can. This is the absolute key step in the process.

In fact, if you just took this one step on-board, as a general rule without specifying what you want, you would see your life begin to naturally upgrade time and again, as the Law of Attraction responds to your positive magnetic presence. It's great to practice just feeling consistently upbeat and happy because, when you do pick something you want and decide to be more specific, you'll already be on a good vibrational frequency, to springboard forwards towards getting what you want.

POSITIVE THINKING

If you've read other books, or watched videos, about the Law of Attraction, you'll have probably come across the advice to think in a more positive way, by using positive affirmations, by swapping out negative words for positive ones, by switching your mind-set to optimism, and by talking to yourself in a kinder inner voice. Of course, this is great advice for any reason. Positive thinking makes us feel good, and that's the whole point, we all just want to feel good. In terms of the Law of Attraction, positive thinking will naturally lead you to positive feeling.

The key here is to make sure you're using positive statements, not double negative statements. Basically cut out words like 'not, don't, and can't'. The feeling of 'not wanting' to feel a certain way doesn't translate on a vibrational level, you would be focusing your energy on the negative feeling instead of replacing it with the opposite, positive feeling you actually want to feel.

So instead of thinking or saying 'I don't want to do this job anymore...' and focusing on your current experience of hating your job, which will keep you in that job, and attract to you more of the same frustration, replace it with the job you do want to have, and imagine yourself working in that job now. Simply imagine the experience of this other job you would prefer, think and say 'I am happy working as a...', and 'a typical day of work includes...'

It's important to let go of the 'if, when, and some-day' mentality, like 'if I was paid a higher salary, I would...', 'when my boss finally praises me for doing a good job, then...', or 'some day when I have a better job I will feel...', and translate that into the present tense. This is because you need to be on that high vibrational frequency now, in the present, in order to send that message out to the universe and get the Law of Attraction working on it.

You can begin by identifying what you don't want if that's what you want to change, but then get away from that negative vibrational frequency by stepping into the opposite.

Any time you catch yourself complaining, or feeling hard done by, switch your negative vibration off. Think differently if you can, try to find the positive or the lesson you're learning from your situation, or simply put some music on, get some exercise, and literally shift your energy out of the state you're in.

Nothing will change if you focus on the state you're currently in, you have to direct your positive energy to where you want to go.

POSITIVE FEELING

The words themselves are irrelevant. It's what these words mean to you and how they make you FEEL that matters. It's great to change your vocabulary from negative to positive, it's an effective tool that moves you in the right direction, but positive thinking isn't the key to the Law of Attraction, despite what you may have come to believe. The key is positive feeling. The key is getting into a state of emotional vibration that matches the vibration of what you want.

So, in terms of this new job scenario, you could focus on the feeling you get from a higher salary, or more freedom, more time with your loved ones, feeling appreciated, valued, and praised for doing a good job. Flood yourself with the feelings that this other job would give you. We all enjoy different aspects of our work, so make sure you're really being specific here, and not stepping into how just anyone would feel.

Think about how you will feel when you experience having what you want in your life. What is the ultimate FEELING you're seeking by having it? Like positive words, the object or 'thing' you want is also fairly irrelevant. What matters is how the object or 'thing' makes you feel. After all, THAT'S WHY YOU WANT IT.

That's why you need to concentrate your efforts on the FEELING in order to attract whatever it is that gives you that FEELING. However, we don't all feel the same way about the same things.

YOURS IS A UNIQUE EXPERIENCE

Most of us want many of the same things, but having these things doesn't give us the same feeling. This is why mimicking someone else's path to success won't necessarily work for you.

Let's look at money, for example. People react to money and material possessions in different ways. Some think of money as a bad thing, they attach negative connotations to consumerism, capitalism, the cause of all that's wrong in the world. All that negativity means they reject money from flowing into their life, whether they're conscious of it or not. Some think there's only so much to go around, so if they're greedy there won't be enough for other people, but this simply isn't true.

This life is abundant. You can have as much of anything you want, and there are many people out there who are living proof of that. If they can have it, so can you. There's an endless supply of anything you can imagine. The Law of Attraction says so. Don't be fooled by social conditioning.

Once you have everything you want, what you do with it is up to you. If you suddenly had an abundant flow of money into your life, there's nothing to stop you from sharing it with others, with charities, with the less fortunate, or investing into something that helps people in another way. It's all about your chosen perspective.

For me, money means freedom, adventure, a carefree lifestyle that can take me travelling anywhere in the world; whereas, for my mum, money makes her feel stable, secure, and if she had enough to buy a property she would have a safe settled place to be. So to manifest money into my life, I would focus on the feeling of freedom, spontaneity, feeling light and carefree. While my mum would need to focus on safety, stability, and feeling grounded.

You can't follow the exact same process as someone else and expect to achieve the same results. Attracting one of these things into my life or yours doesn't cause the same feeling for both of us, so we each need to fine tune our own vibrational frequency.

You have to tailor your process to your own personal preferences, take control and take responsibility for how you feel today and every day, then reap the rewards that are also specific to you. No two people have the same experience no matter how similar it looks from the outside.

STATE OF LACK

The main objective here is to feel how you want to feel, now. If you've been advised to practice detachment, to think of what you want then let it go, it's not about seeing what you want as if you no longer want it, it's about getting into the state of vibration as if you already have it now, and therefore have no need for the vibration of 'wanting' or being in that state of lack or living with the absence of that thing. That's confusing, I know.

If you had the thing you want now, you would no longer be in the state of wanting it. You would no longer be in a state of lack, of absence, of not having that thing in your life. The Law of Attraction is based on how you feel. If you feel that sense of wanting, of not having, you will continue to want and experience lack. If you can move into the vibrational state of feeling like you have that thing you want, you will attract the experience of having it.

It is tricky, and it does take some practice, but once you get into the rhythm of feeling however it is you want to feel, the Law of Attraction can become an effortless life tool you can tap into anytime, anywhere.

If I had all the money I needed, I would feel free. So by feeling free now, as if I do have the money I need now, I move into the vibrational state of freedom, which attracts the hard evidence into my life that supports me feeling that way – more money. By feeling how money would make me feel now, by truly feeling it with every fibre of my being, I already achieve the effect more money would bring me.

By feeling free now, I no longer NEED the thing that makes me feel that way, so I naturally let go of the lack of that feeling and therefore the lack of what causes that feeling – more money. So yes, you have to let go of something, but that comes naturally. By truly believing in how you feel, right now in the present, you will automatically detach from that state of lack.

'But, Kerry, how do I feel the effect of something I don't have the cause to feel?'

You make use of your ingrained super power – your imagination. Our natural ability to imagine something that doesn't already exist is incredible, magical, and extremely powerful. You always have the option to imagine a reality entirely different to the one you believe you're experiencing.

In any given moment, you can choose to see things a different way. You can switch from having a bad day to a good day, and vice versa, simply by interpreting things the opposite way. If something doesn't go the way you wanted it to, you can choose to be annoyed, you can choose to see it as a lesson, or you can choose to see it making way for something better. When someone or something leaves your life, you have the choice to see it as making space in your life to be filled with good things, with something or someone else. You always have a choice. You always have a choice in how you interpret what you experience, what you attach meaning to, and how you choose to react or respond every moment of every day. There are always at least two different options.

In terms of the Law of Attraction, you really can get into a state of bliss by simply focusing all your attention on imagining how you want to feel and flooding yourself with that feeling whenever you remember to. The more you practice feeling good, behaving in a positive way, and living with an upbeat attitude, the easier and more natural it gets. The more you live in this high vibrational frequency the more good fortune you'll attract.

WHY THINGS DON'T CHANGE

It is so common for people to get caught up in a state of frustration, and disappointment, fixated on what they don't like in their current reality. Some people seem to love drama, love confrontation, love a challenge, or love an argument. Those people will get plenty more of the same. By complaining, talking about all the negativity they experience, and spreading more of that vibration around them, the more they'll attract negative experiences that support the state they're in.

The Law of Attraction is still working in these cases and, if it could think, it would probably think it was doing a good job. It speaks a language of vibrations and it's responding perfectly to everything you're focusing on. What's the problem?

The Law of Attraction will lead those people towards more of the same, effectively blocking them from receiving the kind of life they want, because they're so fixated on not having it, because they're not sending out a clear vibrational message that they want anything different.

THE FEELING OF GRATITUDE

So, consistently focusing on not having enough of something, will bring you more experiences of not having enough of it. Focusing on the lack of something, the absence of something, triggers the universe to say,

'Yes, here's the thing you're focused on. You obviously like it so much that I'll give you more. Here's another reason for you to keep feeling that way'.

Instead, focus on the gratitude for the fact that you always get what you need, you always have enough to survive, and see that as a blessing. When times get hard the universe finds some way to provide for you, even if it turns up like a miracle at the last stressful minute. No matter where you are in life, be grateful to be here today, to have survived all the challenges you've faced, and be grateful that you've had support every step of the way in one form or another.

Focusing on how grateful, lucky, or fortunate you feel in any moment, whenever possible, will attract more good fortune into your life. Practicing gratitude will attract more reasons for you to feel gratitude. That's why some people seem lucky to the rest of us, they're in flow with the Law of Attraction. They're grateful for whatever they have, no matter how much it is, and the universe says,

'Oh you like that, do you? Here's some more.'

'Well, thank you very much. I feel so lucky, and blessed, and grateful.'

'Well in that case, you should have some more...'

I'm sure you get it by now. It's a vibrational thing. Gratitude is a lovely frequency of positive vibration. It's the exact feeling you're reaching for, the feeling you'll have when you get what you want. So gratitude is up there with the other high vibe feelings of happiness, excitement, and joy.

EXERCISES TO HELP YOU FEEL IT

SUGGESTED MEDITATIONS

HERE AND NOW

This is a meditation to get you out of the past and future, and bring you into the here and now. Sit comfortably, upright, and close your eyes. As you inhale, imagine a beam of white light coming down from the sky into the crown of your head and travelling into the core of your being, perhaps the heart or solar plexus. As you inhale and imagine this, also think 'I am here'. As you exhale, imagine this light spreading outwards through the whole of your body and out into your surroundings. As you exhale and imagine this, also think 'I am now'. Repeat this practice for as long as you like, you could set a gentle timer alarm for five or ten minutes if you want to.

FLOOD YOURSELF WITH FEELING

This meditation is a way of experiencing a feeling in the present, not prompted by having what you want, but simply recognising the power you have to feel however you want to feel in any moment. Sit comfortably, upright, and close your eyes. Allow the mind chatter to fade away, perhaps beginning with the 'here and now meditation' until you feel fully present. Focus your attention inside your body and notice how you feel, where that feeling lives, and breathe into the place. Then from the core of your being, your heart or solar plexus, flood your body with the feeling you want to feel - like joy, excitement, or a calm state of bliss, for example. Imagine this feeling as a ball of light energy, and then spread it throughout your body and into your surroundings, really embracing it with every inch of your being. Repeat this practice until it feels real to you, until you truly feel how you want to feel, or set a timer like before and make this a regular practice you can tap into at any time.

SUGGESTED JOURNALING

Now that you've decided what you want, I want you to think about why you want it. How would having what you want make you feel? Try free flow writing, by writing what you want at the top of the page and allowing yourself to write about the feelings you attach to it, how your life would change, how the people in your life would respond, and how you would feel about that. You may need to identify how not having it makes you feel now so that you can move in the direction of the opposite positive feeling. Don't get stuck in this place of lack, just use it as a springboard over the fence into the feeling you want to feel by having it. That's the place you want to be in.

If you prefer you can draw a brainstorm or mind-map, by writing what you want in the middle of the page and drawing connecting lines to your feelings and responses to it, like a spider and its legs, or colourful bubbles. You can even doodle little sketches to go with the feelings and scenarios that come up.

SUGGESTED QUESTIONS

How would having what you want make you feel?
What else in your life now gives you that feeling?
What have you had before that made you feel that way?
Is there anything you can do to make yourself feel that way now?

SUGGESTED GRATITUDE PRACTICE

Make a list of the things you're grateful to have now. For each thing, think about why you're grateful for it, and which feelings are connected to it. How does having it make you feel? How would not having it make you feel?

Now move across to this thing you want, that you're focusing this process on. Add it to your list as if you have it now. Express gratitude for it, think about why you're grateful for it, and which feelings are connected to it. How does having it make you feel? How does not having it make you feel? Compare the items on this gratitude list and identify any similarities. Do you lean towards certain feelings? Is there an overriding theme? Are you seeking different things to get the same feeling? Would these things actually create that feeling for you, or can you create it for yourself? Is there anything you can do now to change any negative feelings into positive ones?

Consider, also, the possibility of having what you want, think about the position you're in and the ability you have to reach that place of having it. Express gratitude for all of the resources available to you that will help you have what you want, express gratitude for the support you have from the universe, for the Law of Attraction working with you to get what you want, for the people you can depend upon as you embark on this journey and face challenges. Who would you go to for support in particular scenarios? Express gratitude for them too, and express gratitude for yourself – for showing up, for committing to do this work, for putting yourself first, for making what you want a priority, and for simply being you.

Chapter Seven

STEP 3 - DESERVE IT

Do you love yourself enough to know you are worth it, that you deserve everything you want?

SO YOU'VE DECIDED what you want, and you've learnt to flood yourself with the feeling it gives you. That excited overjoyed sense of having it will put you in a happy vibrational state, on the same frequency as what you want and, over time, hard evidence will turn up to cause you to feel more of that same feeling. At its simplest level this is how the Law of Attraction works, like attracts like. Choosing to feel happy as often as you can attracts more happiness.

There shouldn't be anything holding you back now, from getting what you want. I say there shouldn't be because, for some of us, there will still be something in the way. Lots of us, consciously or unconsciously, believe we don't deserve what we want.

WHY DON'T YOU ALREADY HAVE IT?

We've allowed ourselves to believe it takes hard work to get to where we want to be, and we haven't put in enough work yet. We've allowed ourselves to believe that other people were born lucky, or they're better than us, more worthy of good fortune. We've allowed ourselves to believe that someday, when this, or that, changes, when we pass this, or that, milestone, when we get validation from this, or that, person, when we're finally told, and believe ourselves, that we're good enough, we'll deserve to get what we want.

It's a lack of self-worth, which tends to go fairly unnoticed in most of our daily lives. It affects our self-confidence, our self-belief, our self-esteem, and even our self-care. We rush through the day on autopilot, doing what needs to be done, serving others, and rarely giving ourselves a second thought. You might have low self-worth, be lacking in self-love, and be completely oblivious to it.

Seriously, the most likely reason you don't already have everything you want, is that you don't believe you deserve it. You just don't believe it's possible for you. You believe other people are capable of getting it, but for you, it's different. Why?

POSITIVE COMPARISONS

There is no difference between you and the next person. You are all special, beautiful, very much worthy and deserving, incredibly powerful human beings. You are capable of achieving just as much as anyone else. It doesn't matter how or why, it just is.

There are so many people out there, who have what you want simply because they believe they deserve it, because they have the confidence to go after it, because they back themselves, because they play for their own team, and they believe in their ability to win. Sometimes, that's all it takes.

There are examples, in every field, of people achieving more than other people expect them to, of reaching heights no one thought possible. It doesn't just come down to talent, or intelligence, or beauty. The pivotal tip of the balance is that these other people have high levels of self-worth. They believe they deserve the world, and SO DO YOU.

RULES & RESTRICTIONS

If you know what you want but don't believe you deserve it, this whole process will be blocked by that feeling of unworthiness, of not being good enough to have it. You'll hold yourself back from having what you want, you won't move in that direction, because you're not a vibrational match to it. Whatever rules and restrictions you've set yourself up with need to be addressed because, until you believe you deserve what you want, you'll be emitting a low vibrational frequency that actually rejects it.

If you catch yourself thinking 'I'll be happy when...' or 'I'll be able to reach that next level, or upgrade, once I...' and those statements act like a criticism of who you are today, you're setting yourself up with blocks.

If those statements feel positive and motivational, like your intuition is prompting you to move in the direction of your dream, like you've had inspired instructions that will take you from A to B, that's fine, take those steps and move on up. But if they're holding you back and covering up an underlying belief that you're not good enough yet, that you're undeserving of something, then you need to do some work on your self-worth.

As soon as you do think you're worthy of it, as soon as you step up to that standard you think you need to be on to receive everything you want, the universe will say yes and prove it with hard evidence. Your experience of reality always supports your beliefs.

SELF-CARE

Some of us grew up unaware of the benefits of a simple structured routine. Perhaps there wasn't a good role model to set the example of how to practice self-love and self-care, and the old cliché applies – we don't know what we don't know.

Maybe parents worked too hard, had their priorities in the wrong order, or were absent. Sometimes children have experienced being bottom of the list, the last priority, which teaches them to put themselves last as adults too. Whatever the circumstances, something gets missed in the self-care education.

Self-care is not as widely practiced as it should be, and it's not something that gets discussed openly because there's an assumption that most of us of the same culture are all living the same kind of daily life behind closed doors, including daily routines and self-care habits. This simply isn't true.

Plenty of people neglect their own needs in favour of others, they let their personal hygiene slip or do the bare minimum, they might only make an effort with their appearance for other people, not for themselves, shying away from mirrors at home, and they think they can't afford to spend the time or money on treating themselves to what they really need, but consider a luxury.

You are the most important person in your life.

If you would spend that time or money on someone else, on someone you love, you should be willing to also spend just as much on yourself, and you should be spending it on yourself first, before them.

You are a gift. You give so much to everyone else that you need to regularly replenish your source of energy and love. You need to be full to the brim with self-love, before you convert that to loving energy for everyone else. Otherwise you'll run out, you'll get to the point where you have nothing more to give.

Self-care practices are different for everyone, and they upgrade over time as you become more comfortable with them. Many of us need to start with simply meeting our basic needs, like showering or bathing daily, making an effort to look and feel good even if we're home alone, doing it for ourselves, getting enough sleep, eating well, not punishing ourselves with negative self-talk, and choosing a patient and kind inner voice. All of these things are connected; our self-care practices affect our mental, emotional, and physical health.

Once we get comfortable with meeting basic needs we can move up to treating ourselves like we treat others, buying ourselves flowers or presents, taking ourselves out for coffee or lunch, keeping our home clean and tidy for ourselves like we would if we had a guest coming round. Whatever you would do for someone else, do it for yourself. You deserve it too.

Then the fun really starts. Then you can begin to love yourself so much that you would treat yourself even better than you would treat someone else. You might start booking massages and expensive beauty treatments that you wouldn't have done before, you might take yourself on holiday or to a retreat of some kind, with or without other people, you might decide to invest in your own future, book a course or go back to school and train in that profession you always wanted to learn.

The possibilities are endless when you realise that you are truly the most important person in your life, that you deserve all the love you give to others, that there isn't a limit to how much love you have to give as long as you keep filling yourself up first.

The Law of Attraction really does work as a law of nature, of like attracting like, so the more love you experience, by giving it to yourself, the more love you'll experience giving and receiving around others.

Do you see how you can upgrade your life in stages like this? You can improve your self-care and self-worth habits a little at a time, until you get to a place of treating yourself to a pretty luxurious lifestyle. You'll get there, but it's up to you to make it happen.

As a side note, there will be other people with low self-worth, who find it hard to experience the love you try to give them because they don't believe they deserve it. You can't change that by showering them with more love, and depleting your own resources, but you can show them how to love themselves too, by setting the example. You can talk openly about how you're raising your self-worth and, even if they argue with you, they will be taking it in, and thinking about it later.

Just remember that you had to do this yourself, and they have to do that too. We each have a responsibility to ourselves to show ourselves love. We each have to learn our own lessons, and we can't do that work for someone else. Just bear that in mind and be patient as the people around you are affected by the changes they see. The love will ripple outwards over time.

GETTING HELP

You might have a lot of work to do in this area, more than you first realise. We all have on-going life lessons to learn as we grow, age and evolve. The learning never ends. If you really want to commit to doing this work on your self-worth there are plenty of professionals, coaches, spiritual guides, books, courses, retreats, therapists, and counsellors ready and waiting to support you.

RAISING MY SELF WORTH

The biggest obstacle I had to face in my Law of Attraction process was raising my self-worth, and believing that I truly deserved what I wanted, which is why this step absolutely had to be included. It's the turning point for so many people. Understanding the Law of Attraction, and going through the motions of simply applying it as a process, wasn't enough for me. I had to be ready and able to receive everything I was asking for.

Through working on myself in other ways, paying particular attention to what some call shadow work, I began to learn that I had incredibly low levels of self-worth.

This kept showing up as the core reason why I felt unable to go after anything I wanted. I was convinced, at a deep subconscious level, that there was something wrong with me. I believed I didn't deserve the love, money or success that I so desperately wanted, and the reason I was so desperate for it, was that I was withholding it from myself, thus creating a catch-22 cycle, of wanting and resisting the same things, over and over.

The Law of Attraction supported my beliefs by delivering hard evidence that I was no-one's priority, that I deserved to be treated a certain way, that I wasn't a romantic catch, that career-wise, despite being told repeatedly that I was talented and top of my game, I dipped in and out of day jobs, allowing others to benefit from my talents, supporting other people's dreams and not my own. I didn't put myself forward for what I really wanted to do, I dabbled with my dream as if it was a hobby, and I continued to experience a dissatisfying life, which was what I unknowingly believed I deserved.

As I increased my self-worth, through shadow work, through understanding my inner child, through setting loving boundaries and rejecting any treatment less than what I learnt to be my new standard, my life went through a mysterious upgrade. The people and places that had been inaccessible to me before suddenly began to seek my presence. I received invitations left and right, and had to keep pinching myself as my life took on the miraculous qualities of a dream.

Nothing about me had physically changed. I wasn't earning more money, or dressing differently. I hadn't become someone other than who I had always been, my status hadn't been raised, and I didn't get a promotion or have any reason why, externally, I might come across as more important in any way. Yet, internally I had stepped up higher in my self-worth, I had learnt to believe I deserved better than I had previously allowed myself to receive, and better suddenly began to turn up.

It felt like overnight success but, of course, such a thing doesn't exist. The moment when everything changes is actually the moment you NOTICE everything has changed.

I had been going through a lifelong process towards that point, the momentum had been building over time, slowly, incrementally, raising my self-worth a little bit at a time, until I reached the level of belief that I was worthy of what I wanted. Now, I'm simply watching it all rush into my life, doing my part of the teamwork by feeling as great as I want to feel, and following my intuition like a treasure map plotted just for me.

EXERCISES TO HELP YOU DESERVE IT

SUGGESTED MEDITATIONS

LOVING MEDITATION

Sit comfortably, upright, and close your eyes. Then wrap your arms around yourself and sit in a warm loving self-hug while you meditate. As you inhale, imagine a beam of pink loving light coming down from the sky through the crown of your head, and down to your heart. As you inhale and imagine this light, also think 'I am loved'. As you exhale, imagine this light spreading outwards through the whole of your body and out into your surroundings. As you exhale and imagine this light, also think 'I am loving'. Repeat this practice for as long as you like, you could set a gentle timer alarm for five or ten minutes if you want to.

DESERVE THE WORLD

This is a grounding meditation, to connect you with the loving Mother Earth that loves and supports you. You deserve her love, you deserve everything she gives you, you deserve to be here, and you deserve to thrive and flourish like everything else on this planet.

Sit comfortably, upright, and close your eyes. As you inhale, imagine a beam of green loving light coming down from the sky through the crown of your head, down through your third eye, and throat, to your heart. As you exhale, imagine this light travelling down, through your solar plexus, to where you connect with the earth and imagine tree roots growing from you into the earth, it doesn't matter how or where.

Repeat this practice for as long as you like, focusing on a warm loving feeling travelling through the central line of your body into the earth. You could set a gentle timer alarm for five or ten minutes if you want to.

If you enjoy this practice and become skilled at the flow of energy travelling through you from sky to earth, you can go a step further and imagine those roots going all the way through the earth and back into the sky, just as it does. Everything is connected, the earth, the sky, the stars, and you. We all have a place in this universe. We are the universe.

SUGGESTED JOURNALING

Try writing a letter to yourself, giving yourself advice, giving yourself uncensored opinions, commenting on your day, or something that happened recently. Try adding in compliments, praise, and constructive criticism. Then read it back, aloud if you like. How much of that letter sounds like your inner voice? How much of it is positive or negative? Would you talk to someone you love that way? What do you need to change about the way you talk to yourself?

Now write a letter to your inner child, to your past child self. Tell that child what they needed to hear at the time, tell them you understand, that it's over now, comfort them, reassure them, tell them the grown up you is here now to handle the grown up stuff, tell them they don't need to worry anymore, tell them they can play. Then do something playful, put some music on and dance, sing, or do whatever you liked to do as a child.

SUGGESTED QUESTIONS

Consider those other people who have what you want. What makes them different to you? What is it about them, which you think sets them apart? What have you decided makes them more deserving of what you want, than you? What do you believe about these other people that you don't believe about yourself?

What do you think they believe about themselves that gets them what they want? Do they think they're too much of this or that, and not enough of whatever else? Or do they believe in themselves, do they believe they're entitled to have what they have?

What can you change about your beliefs, regarding yourself and your worth? Where did your negative beliefs come from, and do they still stand now? Have you ever questioned why you believe what you believe about yourself? Question it now.

SUGGESTED GRATITUDE PRACTICE

What are you grateful for about yourself? Don't be modest - really go to town on this exercise. No one has to see this list if you're shy, this can just be for you. So, cover every angle, your loving nature, your cleanliness, your punctuality, your loyalty, your habit of picking snails off the wet pavement so they don't get crunched underfoot, your physical features, cute toes, extra hairy armpits, your singing in the shower, your sewing skills, your university degree, your obsession with cassette tapes, whatever you like about yourself, whatever you're grateful for.

Do the same for others - what would your friends, family, colleagues, pets, even kitchen utensils, say they were grateful for about you? Do some of these things match out of what you think and what they think? Are you really seeing yourself how they do?

Then list what you're grateful about your friends, family, kitchen utensils, and see what qualities they have that you actually have too, qualities you weren't able to see in yourself before. Add those to your own list.

Give yourself a hug and thank yourself for being you.

Chapter Eight

STEP 4: KNOW IT

*Sometimes just switching the word 'believe'
for 'know' is enough. I know my dreams exist.
I know they're out there waiting for me.*

S O YOU'VE DECIDED what you want, you've uncovered the feeling you're actually seeking, and you accept that you deserve to have it. Now I want you to know it's out there, that it exists, not just believe in a possibility really KNOW it's a real thing that IS going to happen. Let's think about what you believe, what you know, and what the difference is.

BELIEVING VS. KNOWING

The word 'believe' has lost its meaning over the years, and while you may have been advised to believe in the possibility of your manifestations becoming real, my understanding of this process was flipped on its head when I stopped believing and started KNOWING.

There's a difference between believing in things and knowing them to be true. Children believe in Santa Claus, the Tooth Fairy, monsters under the bed, etc. Adults believe in God, superstition, good and bad fortune, karma, etc. These are things we can't see but choose to believe in, for one reason or another. They're invisible, we have no sensory proof of them, we have chosen to accept what we've been told or taught by others, and we've chosen to believe in them.

What else is invisible in our lives? What else have we been told or taught exists even though we don't necessarily see any proof? What about electricity, the internet, gravity, photosynthesis, meditation, germs, or mental health conditions? Do we believe in them, or KNOW they're real? Can you now see the difference between believing in something, and knowing something exists?

Believing and knowing are also two different vibrational frequencies. They tell the universe two different messages about the same thing. Beliefs leave room for doubt, leave room for change, and leave room for evidence to the contrary. Knowledge doesn't.

Do you still believe Santa Claus is going to turn up with a sack load of presents and the thing you want might or might not be in there, depending on how good you've been, depending on whether Santa even exists? No, the threat or promise of Santa doesn't get to dictate how you behave anymore, or what you get in return.

You're an adult now and this is your life. You can choose to take ownership, take responsibility, take control, and tell the universe exactly who you are and what you'll stand for. You have the power. That's the kind of conviction you're aiming for here.

'I know who I am, I know what I want, I know it exists, and I know it is mine.'

TURN BELIEVING INTO KNOWING

If you believe you're capable of achieving your dreams, goals and ambitions, you will have the motivation to make it happen. If you believe you aren't capable of it, you won't. It's like Henry Ford said,

'Whether you believe you can or you can't, you're right.'

We always have to begin by believing in something, before it has any chance of becoming possible, right? We have to believe in ourselves, in our ability and, most of all, in the potential reality of something happening.

It always begins with belief. Your beliefs affect everything you do, say, the way you behave, and the way you interpret your life experiences. What you believe to be real, what you believe you deserve, and what you believe is possible defines who you are and the way you choose to live.

What you believe plays a big part in how you experience life, it defines who you are as a person and colours your approach to any situation you face. Don't get me wrong, your beliefs are important. You're entitled to your beliefs. You have the choice of what you have faith in, and no one can take that away from you. The choice is yours.

All I'm saying is that beliefs, rather than knowledge, are concepts that haven't been proven or disproven. You might read something, experience something, have a conversation with someone and feel triggered to question your beliefs.

Taking responsibility for the beliefs you choose to keep or cast aside can be life-changing, and that's an exercise in itself, but when it comes to working with the Law of Attraction, simply believing in a possibility leaves room for doubt.

By wishing, waiting, even expecting, you are reaffirming the state of lack, the absence of the thing, the belief that you don't already have it. This will just keep it at arms-length. Until you KNOW it is yours, right now, you will stop yourself from seeing it in physical existence. It will always sit out of reach, round the corner, out of sight, waiting for you to simply acknowledge it.

If you BELIEVE in something, you're not 100% sure of it, there's still the possibility that you might be proven wrong and someone or something could change your mind. But if you KNOW something's true, it's true, and no one can tell you any different.

Beliefs can change at any time, and that determines the vibrational frequency they emit. That frequency is pretty strong, but not as strong as the frequency of KNOWING something to be true, without a shadow of a doubt, and that's where I want you to get to.

I want you to KNOW that what you want EXISTS. I want you to KNOW that what you want is out there in the world, I want you to KNOW the universe has your back, and I want you to KNOW the Law of Attraction is willing to work in your favour. I want you to transform your beliefs into KNOWLEDGE.

I want the universe to respond to you as solidly and substantially as the vibrational frequency you're sending out. I want you to stop just believing in a possibility, and become absolutely certain that what you want already exists, that it's out there somewhere, that it's yours, and that it's meant for you.

STEP BY STEP PROCESS

If you find it tricky to turn your belief into knowledge, you can approach this with a step by step process to convince your naturally sceptical mind that what you want exists.

First of all, the fact that you want something at all means you're able to imagine it, right? Your imagination is based on experiential information; what you've seen, heard, touched, tasted, and felt over the course of your life provides the content for your imagination. This can include what seems impossible, after all inventors create the impossible every day. It depends what you're trying to achieve for yourself.

Now I'm going to make a guess here and assume that you probably want something someone else has, so the fact that someone else has it definitely means it exists. They have it. It exists. It exists for them, and the fact you can witness the existence of it at all, surely backs up your knowledge that it exists. It's real. It's possible. You can have it too.

The more you focus on what you want, the more you're going to attract hard evidence of it in your reality. You're going to see what you want all over the place. Friends, family, even strangers, will all seem to have it, and this is the really sticky point; don't let yourself fall into the trap of feeling negative jealousy or envy.

JEALOUSY

Seeing other people get what you want is a good thing. The more you're provided with evidence that what you want exists, the closer you are to having it yourself.

So if your friends, rivals, or business competitors seem to be ahead of you, if they seem to be achieving what you want while you're not, don't take the bait and get jealous, applaud them. Express gratitude for the proof that what you want is within reach, express gratitude for the proof that people just like you are getting what they want, just like you will. Express gratitude and the universe will say,

'Oh you like that, do you? You want that too?'

Stay on track in your positive vibration, take these

scenarios you've witnessed as hard evidence that your dream exists, it's out there, and it's almost under your nose! This experience in itself should convince you that you don't just believe it's possible, you KNOW it's possible. You've seen it, heard it, and felt it with your own senses.

The universe is always listening, waiting for that prompt from you to tell it how to react. If you maintain that positive attitude, that positive frequency, and you declare again,

'Yes, I want that. I know there's one out there, waiting for me too. I trust the universe to guide me to get it, and I know I'll get mine just as soon as I'm ready,'

The universe will guide you to getting yours. But if you switch from your happy positive frequency to a jealous negative frequency, all the universe will hear from you is,

'I reject the experience that person is having. Keep it away from me.'

And the universe says,

'Alright, I hear you, loud and clear; none of that for you.'

THE LAND OF DESIRE

If you connect a negative emotion to what you want, you're going to communicate that it's become something you don't want, it's something that repels you, and the Law of Attraction will respond in kind. Instead, choose to accept that the more you are seeing what you want around you, the closer you're moving towards it. It's like you're walking into the land of that desire, where everyone has one, and soon you will too. You'll find yours, if you just keep going.

The point is to not doubt your desire, to not question the possibility of you having it. You have to convince yourself that there will come a day that you will get there. You'll be ready to have whatever it is you want. In fact, it already belongs to you, it's yours, no matter whether you physically see it or not. It's out there somewhere.

In your own time, and when you're ready to, you'll do your part of the work to move in its direction, find it, and stake your claim on it.

On top of that, the fastest way to attract what you want is to KNOW you have it, right now, regardless of any evidence to the contrary. It takes some serious imaginative and emotional power to get onto, and maintain, that strong vibrational frequency, but it does speed up the process if you can get the hang of it.

By tapping into the feeling you want to feel right now, that feeling you'll get by having what you want, you basically already have what you're reaching for. Truly knowing you have your desire right now in the present, unaffected by any limitations, or restrictions, of your current reality, can make the whole Law of Attraction process happen at warp speed. It might defy logic, but it does happen. The universe will provide the hard evidence that supports the way you feel.

MANIFESTING

Like the concept of believing in something, in order to make it happen, manifesting has become an equally popular and overused word in recent years. This concept also goes against the vibrational state of KNOWING something exists and that it's meant for you.

You're not trying to manifest something out of thin air, you're not trying to conjure up a magic trick or illusion, you're not a God creating and destroying worlds, you're not performing some kind of miracle. Our use of the term manifesting and manifestation gives the impression that understanding and working with the Law of Attraction will give us some kind of otherworldly fantasy power to pluck rabbits out of hats or turn people into frogs. It doesn't work like that.

Manifestation, when you really get to know it, is the point in time when you align with what you want and see it before you. It takes groundwork, it takes knowledge, and understanding, of the process, and it takes movement, towards upgrade after upgrade, as you move up onto the vibrational frequency of what you want.

OTHER PEOPLE MAKE IT LOOK EASY

It's not that difficult once you know how to work with the universe, and get into the flow of the Law of Attraction. It can seem like a surprise to see something you wanted manifest, but if you look back over the journey you've taken to get there, you'll see that you did play your part, you did do the work that was needed, and you did follow your intuition in the right direction.

Please don't misunderstand these terms that have convinced so many that the Law of Attraction is some kind of magic trick, that it will bring you miraculous instant gratification. You'll only get there when you step into the same vibrational frequency of what you want, and maintain it. That can be done in an instant, but it takes practice.

There are definitely people out there making it work like instant gratification, who have practiced so much that they slip in and out of vibrational frequencies barely with a second thought to how they do it. There are also some people who grew up, making the universe work for them, completely unaware of any of this technical, behind-the-scenes information.

Just like anything else, there are always anomalies, and there are always people who are seemingly born with this innate understanding for one reason or another, and there are some who have it channelled through them so that they can share it with others. These people have even more reason to not just believe in the Law of Attraction. They KNOW it really works.

Again, don't envy these people, be grateful for them. They prove its existence, and they prove you can do what they do too.

EXERCISES TO HELP YOU KNOW IT

SUGGESTED MEDITATION

STRENGTH & CONFIDENCE

This meditation connects you to your solar plexus, the source of your willpower, confidence, and inner strength. The intention is to feel strong in your knowledge that what you want exists and it's meant for you.

Sit comfortably, upright, and close your eyes. As you inhale, imagine a beam of empowering yellow light coming down from the sky through the crown of your head, down through your third eye, down through your throat, and down through your heart, to your solar plexus, just below your ribs. As you exhale, imagine this yellow light as a ball of strong empowering energy growing brighter then spreading outwards through your entire being and out into the air surrounding you.

Repeat this practice for as long as you like, focusing on the feeling of strong empowering confidence. You could set a gentle timer alarm for five or ten minutes if you want to. When you're ready to end the meditation, imagine yourself within a bubble, or circle, of yellow light and breathe a big sigh of release.

SUGGESTED JOURNALING

Write yourself a letter from the universe, directly addressing you, reassuring you that you are held and supported, that the universe has your back, that it knows you're capable of stepping into the life you wish for, that it's guiding you in the right direction all the time, that what you want is out there somewhere waiting for the day when you're ready, that it belongs to you and no one else, that you will get there with perfect timing, exactly when you're meant to. Continue to write in free flow if the inspiration takes you, write with the intention of receiving what the universe wants you to know.

SUGGESTED QUESTIONS

Do you believe, or do you know, you're capable of getting what you want?
Do you believe, or do you know, it already exists?
Do you believe, or do you know, it's out there waiting for you?
What makes you feel this way?
What can you change about your thoughts and actions around this desire to turn believing into knowing, or to make your knowing stronger?

SUGGESTED GRATITUDE PRACTICE

Think about what you want and times when you've seen it in existence, maybe times when you've felt that pang of jealousy seeing other people get what you want. Write a list of those times with the intention of expressing gratitude to the universe, for providing you with the evidence that what you want exists, that what you want is moving closer to you in reality.

Begin each memory with 'Thank you for showing me

the existence of ...' then describe the memory you have of experiencing it. Finish your list by writing 'Thank you for bringing me closer to getting what I want.'

FULL MOON MANIFESTATION RITUALS

Many people follow the lunar cycle as a guide to understanding the ebb and flow of how they're feeling in connection to the phases of the moon. The moon has such a significant impact on our world that it makes sense that it would affect us too.

You may have already come across the concept of full moon ceremonies and manifestation rituals in conjunction with the moon. It might seem like a mysterious practice that other people do, something you don't know how to do for yourself, but it can be as simple as you want to make it. You can hold your own ritual and harness the support of this law of nature at home, by yourself.

You'll need to find out when the next full moon is, prepare yourself with some pieces of paper, a pen, fire and water; so perhaps a candle or even a lighter, and a glass of water.

The key is to write two short lists, or just two things, on paper. Write what you want to release or let go of, and on a separate piece of paper write what you want to call in or invite into your life. Read each one aloud, addressed to the universe. If you want to, you can thank the universe for helping you release and invite these specific things. Then carefully burn and submerge each piece of paper in water. It's as simple as that.

You might like to add a list of people you forgive,

writing out what you forgive them for, and how you now understand why they did what they did. If you choose to add a forgiveness list, make sure to include forgiveness for yourself.

You might like to set up a special area for your full moon ritual, with crystals or precious keepsakes, perhaps meditate in the space before and/or after, and even give yourself a card reading if that's something you do. You can also use this time to communicate with your intuition and the universe by journaling and writing out a gratitude list as well. It's your practice, do what feels good to you.

Full moon rituals don't have to be outside, you don't have to be able to see the moon, and they don't have to be anything fancy. It's entirely up to you. You can choose to do this alone or with a friend, or you could decide to join a hosted full moon ritual, online or in your local area. There are lots of people hosting these as social events.

Chapter Nine

STEP 5: WORK IT

There is no shortcut. You still have to do the work, but the work might not be what you thought it was.

So YOU'VE DECIDED what you want, you know the feeling you're trying to get from having it, you've accepted that you deserve it, and now you know it exists and it's out there waiting for you. It's waiting for you to do the work to find it.

GET OFF THE SOFA

This part of the Law of Attraction process works like an invisible treasure map. What you want is out there somewhere, hidden like buried treasure. You know what the treasure is, you know you want it, you know you deserve it, you know how it makes you feel, and you know it exists, you just can't see the map.

Map or not, do you think you'll find buried treasure sitting on the sofa, staying in your house, doing the same things you do every day, changing nothing and going nowhere? Your treasure is out there waiting for you to find it, waiting for you to get up off the sofa, leave the house, take action, and move towards what you want. It's waiting for you to do the work, but the work might not be what you thought it was.

'So what is the work? Where is my treasure? What am I supposed to do now?'

You need answers, right? You need some help, and you need some guidance, because you can't do this thing alone. Luckily for you, you're never alone. The universe has your back. The universe is ready and willing to give you the answers you seek, and it's waiting to guide you whenever you're ready to be guided. Put yourself on the team, be prepared to collaborate, and you will soon find out your team has the map.

Why don't you have the map? Because you're biased, because you don't always know what's best for you, because you can't know in advance that the hardest thing you've ever had to go through will one day be the best thing that ever happened to you. The universe does know what's best for you, it does know when you're going in the right direction, and best of all it can and will tell you.

THE UNIVERSE HAS THE MAP

The universe is your navigator, your co-pilot. Trust it to guide you in the right direction, no matter how much of a detour you seem to be on. Each detour, each scenic route, serves a purpose. It won't always seem like it at the time, but you might be going that way to refuel, or meet someone to join you on your journey, or upgrade your plane so that you can fly higher over some rocky mountains you didn't even see coming. I promise you, the universe knows exactly what it's doing, and where you're going.

If flying a plane isn't a metaphor that works for you, imagine setting your Google Maps App or GPS to take you to a destination while you're walking or driving somewhere. If you couldn't watch the screen, you wouldn't doubt the way you were going, you would listen to the directions and obediently follow them. As you're fed directions, telling you to turn left here, take the third exit there, or stay on this course for five miles, you trust it.

Do that with the universe. Trust it to direct you, trust that it knows where your destination is and how to get there. If you doubt it, or second guess it, you're going to get yourself lost. But if you do get lost, the universe will still bail you out and put you back on the right path, just like a GPS would, with no judgement.

HOW DOES THE UNIVERSE GUIDE YOU?

When you become aware that the universe is communicating with you at all, you might start to notice the strange ways it talks to you. An inspired thought might pop in your head out of the blue, or a friend will randomly tell you exactly what you needed to hear, or you'll notice a street name that reminds you of something, or you'll keep seeing a particular bird or animal, or you'll keep finding red thread everywhere, or you'll have a meaningful dream or conversation, or you'll hear a song playing that seems to be directly talking to you.

Some people find magic in coincidences, and signs, some people use oracle or tarot cards to prompt the universe to talk to them, and some people notice parallel numbers throughout the day, applying numerology or angel numbers, to their particular situation. There are probably just as many ways as there are people, and plenty of people are completely unaware that the universe is talking to them at all.

It could be anything, anywhere, at any time, prompting you to think differently, to reconsider something, to see the lesson in some obstacle, or to move in a different direction. These nudges from the universe will be specific to you, they'll become more common as you become more receptive to them, and only YOU will truly know what they mean to you.

Whatever you attach meaning to means something to you, whatever you feel prompted by, whatever inspires you, whatever triggers you, no matter how silly or meaningless it seems to someone else, is you being guided by the universe. This is how your intuition works.

There are many people out there with heightened intuitive, psychic and holistic abilities, ready and waiting to support others with interpreting signs and messages from the universe. When you want some support and guidance they're a great help, but only you know what rings true in your gut out of what they tell you. You'll be advised to take what resonates and leave the rest. You'll know what the universe is trying to tell you in amongst everything else you see and hear.

However, each of us listens to the universe in our own individual way. We're not all open to the same kind of signs, ideas, challenges, or life lessons. Some people are open to learning through meeting a friend and exploring something together, others are more likely to learn through a romantic partner, and maybe even heartbreak. Some people get flashes of creative inspiration seemingly from nowhere, and some people don't notice these redirections until they look back and realise if they hadn't got on that bus, opened that book, or spilled that cup of coffee, something significant wouldn't have happened.

GO WHERE YOU'RE GUIDED

The universe will lead you in the direction to stumble across that thing you want, or build you up to have it. You might earn it, win it, or start down a new path in life that takes you to its destination. Trust your intuition. If you feel compelled to do something, do it. Co-create with the universe, work with your team and do your part. If it's truly what you want, you'll be willing to do whatever you need to do to get it.

Sometimes you'll notice yourself being guided, and sometimes you won't. It will mostly feel like you're making these decisions yourself, but even the source of your inspirations comes from the universe.

Keep doing what you feel like you should do to move forwards, and you'll be supported to move in the right direction. Then one day, you'll suddenly have what you want, what you asked for, without really knowing how you ended up there. You'll be a new upgraded version of yourself, and this thing you so desperately wanted will be totally ordinary to you, as you find yourself living on a frequency where your dream is an everyday reality.

DO THE GROUNDWORK

When you become aware of how the universe works, how the Law of Attraction is bringing you the experiences you focus on, and how much better your life can be if you play your part and do the work, it can actually be a little overwhelming.

You begin to see the bigger picture, and it seems like there's a hell of a lot of work, and there is, but there's no rush to get it all done. Doing 'the work' on ourselves is a lifelong adventure, which we all undertake, and we all do, whether we know we're doing it or not. The work never ends, and that's what life is all about.

We're constantly learning until the day we die. There's no graduation day where you get your certificate that says you're a completely healed, 100% whole, absolutely issue free, person. So pause, breathe, and relax. All of this so-called work is the work we're all doing throughout our entire lives, aware of it or not.

The difference now is, you have the advantage of being aware of it so you can do your work with intention, with purpose, and with a definite direction. You can evaluate each stage and see where you need to adapt or improve something instead of getting stuck in the cycle of repeating a life lesson like so many others do.

The difference between you and the next person is that you now know what you can do. You can get proactive about it, and you can speed through the life upgrades you're moving towards, faster than someone who's sleepwalking through their life. You have the choice and the power to work with the Law of Attraction, and steer this journey in the direction you want to go. You can accept the lessons you were always going to have to face, and skip through the levels faster with a guide to show you the way.

The Law of Attraction will still be working, it doesn't stop and wait for you to catch up, it never clocks off, so any efforts you make to improve your life, to be more positive, to upgrade little details wherever you can, will all act in your favour and get you moving in the right direction.

Remember, the Law of Attraction has been working behind-the-scenes of your life all along, you just weren't aware that you had control before so, even now, you're consistently seeing results you didn't know you asked for.

GET SOME HELP

Now that you are aware, you have the opportunity to do your part of the work to improve and upgrade your life. The world we live in now is full of resources, guides, coaches, and courses that can help you with any area of your life you want to change.

Consider all of the different memories, traumas, interactions and incidents that are echoing forwards from your past into your experience of this present moment. Your entire perspective is coloured by everything you've been through, possibly changing your angle, your view, and your opinions at each turn.

We actually live our entire lives in our minds, everything we experience is based on how we feel, and we genuinely have complete power over that if we choose to take control and do the work. All that past stuff, bubbling away under the surface of you, can be addressed, can be examined, can be understood afresh, and can have a huge effect on your life. You can let it continue to affect you, or you can choose to work through it. This is what many call doing 'the work'.

Much like you can't help someone who won't accept

help, or help themselves, you need to take responsibility for yourself, for your happiness, for how you interpret and experience your life. If you don't know where to start, reach out and ask for help.

EXERCISES TO HELP YOU WORK IT

SUGGESTED MEDITATIONS

INTUITION MEDITATION

This meditation is designed to connect you with your intuition, to the universal consciousness that talks directly to you.

Focus on the question you want answered, then sit in stillness, comfortably, upright, close your eyes, and clear your mind. Mentally ask the question to the universe from within your mind, then begin meditating.

As you inhale, imagine a beam of intelligent blue light coming down from the sky through the crown of your head, down to your third eye if you're imagining purple, or down to your throat for blue. As you exhale, imagine this light spreading outwards through your entire being and out into the air surrounding you.

Repeat this practice for as long as you like, focusing on the feeling of universal intelligence channelling through you. Bathe in this state of blue light, and listen deeply for the answer to your question.

Ask the question again if you need to, but allow plenty of time for an answer to come. Listen to the empty silence and wait for a message to come through. You will probably be answered through your own thoughts, in your own inner voice, or through visual symbols, colours, or inspired ideas.

When you have your answer write it down in full, and keep writing if more comes through. You might even feel inspired to draw. This is how you've asked the universe to communicate with you, so try not to doubt or resist it. Allow your hand to write or draw freely, and allow the universe to keep talking if it wants to.

SUGGESTED JOURNALING

Shift your focus away from what you can't do and focus on what you can do. The universe will take care of the rest. Write a list of actions you can take today, tomorrow, and next week that will contribute to you moving towards your dream.

If you're struggling to think of anything, you can ask for guidance. Start with a blank page and write a question you want the answer to, even if you don't think you know the answer. Putting your thoughts onto paper makes them real, it gives them substance, and asking these questions will prompt your intuition to speak up.

Now practice free writing, answer the question without too much thought. Allow your pen to drift across the page. Imagine it's not you writing, it's the universe talking to you, giving you all the answers you need right now, the answers you're ready to receive.

Your connection to the universal consciousness will be activated and each time you practice this two-way dialogue, becoming more comfortable with trusting your intuition and the universal consciousness to give you the answers, you will get them.

As you upgrade your life, and move through higher vibrational frequencies, you will probably receive different answers each time you try this exercise, different answers for the different you that you've become.

SUGGESTED QUESTIONS

What can I do to make my dream happen?
What small steps can I take to move towards my dream?
What changes can I make to upgrade my life experience?
How can I make space in my life to allow something new to come in?

SUGGESTED GRATITUDE PRACTICE

Write a list, and express gratitude for, the opportunities you have had, have now, and will have, to take action and upgrade your life by moving forwards in the direction of your dreams.

List the significant moments in your life, the life-changing experiences that put you on the path to where you are today. Express gratitude for your own evolution, for the lessons you've learnt, for the domino effect of events that took you from where you were to where you are today. Acknowledge the ever-changing momentum of your life and the blessings you have had, have now, and will have as you continue to move forwards.

MAKE SPACE IN YOUR LIFE

You can prepare yourself for your dreams to become real. You can make space in your life for this new thing to come in. If you're hoping for the love of your life to turn up, is there room for them in your house, your schedule, your social circle?

You can literally make space for them to enter your life by clearing space in your wardrobe and cupboards for their stuff, by parking your car on one side of the garage to allow for them to park theirs next to it, and you can sleep on one side of the bed leaving the other side available for when they'll soon be sleeping next to you. It might sound silly, but physically making space in their lives for another person has worked for lots of people.

If you want money and success, but you live in a messy cluttered home, you can upgrade your lifestyle right now by changing your environment. Clear that clutter, and get rid of any unnecessary bits and bobs that the more successful you wouldn't live with, or even just tidy them away and hide them from view. You can start upgrading now, in little ways, by choosing more luxurious coloured cushions and visuals that make you feel successful, perhaps framing pictures of friends who inspire you. Think about the kind of homes successful people live in and mimic how they would treat their space; keep your home clean, and raise the standard of how you want to live. As you return home each day to this upgraded environment, you will feel more successful and, as you know, that feeling will attract more of the same.

Seriously, changing your environment to feel luxurious and successful really does work, and it doesn't have to cost much, or anything at all. Just living in a better version of the environment you live in now acts like an upgrade. Just clearing your space to invite in a better lifestyle, and changing your habits to those you would prefer to live with, is a step forwards in itself. You'll trigger that momentum, propel yourself forwards, and actively move in the right direction.

Chapter Ten

THE DISCLAIMER

Embrace the life-changing moments, even the dark ones.
They're always working in your favour.

IT'S BETTER NOT TO KNOW

I HAVE TO ADD a little disclaimer here, on behalf of the universe, before you all start complaining about not getting what you want as soon as you want it. Now that you have all this information about how and why the Law of Attraction works, you're not actually privy to the map that tells you when and where things will happen.

Not knowing this stuff is for your own good. If you knew this information, it would undermine your ability to do the work you need to do to get there. You would try to skip the tough bits. Sometimes it seems like the universe is working against you. It's not.

THE UNIVERSE KNOWS BEST

The universe knows how to move you from where you are to where you want to be. It knows which challenges you need to face to raise your vibration, to change your understanding of something, to upgrade your values, and put you on the same frequency as what you want. The universe knows what's going to transform your life for the better, and it's usually the last thing you expect to have to go through to get there.

What you have to understand, and accept, is that you don't always know best. You don't always know what's good for you. In fact some of the worst experiences we go through in our lives usually end up being the most life-changing lessons, and they prepare us for some of the greatest achievements we later face.

The universe is always acting on behalf of your highest good. The universe truly wants the best for you. Anything you are grateful to have now, whatever circumstances you find yourself in, wherever you are, probably took some work to get to. You know the kind of work I mean now. Think about it.

To meet the vibrational frequency of what you want, the universe will support you in raising your own. This can be a tough, gruelling journey through heartache, struggle, and hardship, but whatever happens, no matter how much you fall, these experiences are always for your highest good.

Sometimes we have to experience certain things in order to prepare us for the life we really want, we have to build a foundation to build our beliefs on, we have to toughen up before we can handle the challenges it will take to get what we want. Trust the universe to do its thing. It really does know what it's doing.

WHEN IT DOES HAPPEN

By the time you actually get what you want, your life will have changed so much that what once seemed like an impossibility has become something easily attained and more of the same is now within your reach. Getting to that place, where your dreams are the new norm for you, can take a lot longer than you want it to, and often people have forgotten what they wished for when it mysteriously turns up.

You might not notice you've got what you wanted, until it suddenly dawns on you or someone points it out, and you have a revelation.

'Oh wow, I forgot I even asked for this. This is exactly what I wanted all that time ago. How did I get from there to here?'

Then you might unpack your vision board from the loft, or flick back through the pages of old journals, to find the time in your life when all this was a magical fantasy far out of your reach. You'll look around yourself at what seems like your ordinary life now and see how much of your experience has upgraded over time.

It's surreal to look back and track your progress from there to here, realising that if you hadn't gone to that place, got on that bus, talked to that person, done that thing, spilled that tea, you wouldn't be here. It's incredible when you get to see how everything lined up perfectly, over time, to lead you to actually have what you wanted.

IT MIGHT GET ROUGH

Whatever comes your way you can handle it. No matter how rough life gets, you will never be given something you're not strong enough to get through. Trust yourself, trust your survival instinct, and trust the temporary nature of everything. Remember, no matter how hard it gets, this too shall pass, and you'll get the chance to evaluate this experience and learn from it.

You'll be thrown challenges designed specifically for you, to move you from one level to the next. If you embrace the nature of that you can give yourself the advantage of being able to learn the lessons quicker, more thoroughly, to understand why you're facing this particular challenge, and you'll know how to tackle it in the way only you can.

Everything happens for a reason, and it happens for your highest good, no matter how devastating it might be at the time.

If you don't want an experience to show up in your life again, face it head on. Invite the lesson in, provoke it to do its worst and tell it to bring it on. There is nothing to be afraid of. You can and will get through anything life throws at you. You always have.

Stand strong no matter hard it gets, and learn from it, once and for all. We all have life lessons to learn and, until we learn them, those lessons will keep repeating themselves. They'll keep showing up in one guise or another, in the people, places, and scenarios we attract ourselves to. The lessons will find us, because no matter how far you run, you can't run away from yourself, or the life you were meant to live.

LOVE

The model of a relationship you witnessed as a child may not fall in line with the healthy loving equal relationship you want and deserve as an adult. Before you can have that you may have to go through some heart-breaking lessons to raise your vibrational frequency, you may have to learn how to live at a higher standard, and treat yourself the way you deserve to be treated. This is why people say 'you have to love yourself first'. The kind of relationship you attract matches your vibrational state.

So to upgrade to the relationship you really want, the universe will take you through a crash course in filtering out the relationships you don't want. You'll be taught to invest in the relationship you have with yourself, increase your self-respect, your self-worth, and change your view of what you're looking for in a partner. You'll be taught this stuff by going through relationships with people who challenge you in the areas you need to look at. It's like training, preparing you for the relationship that inevitably turns up when you're finally ready for it. It takes time.

You might be subconsciously attracting the same partners with certain qualities. You might wonder how, and why, you keep choosing to be with the same kind of person who treats you this way, you'll wonder how you couldn't tell at the start that it would turn out the same way, over and over again.

Every relationship is a lesson, and until you learn that lesson, the universe is going to keep you repeating it. Eventually you'll wake up to what you're being shown, you'll upgrade your standards, you'll replenish your self-worth, you'll reset your boundaries, and you'll finally accept that you deserve more than what you've allowed into your life.

I hopped from relationship to relationship, convinced that I had a type, convinced that I knew what I wanted, and what I deserved. It took a devastating breakup, a complete overhaul of my life as I knew it, to make me do the work on myself. I spent a lengthy amount of time single, learning how to make myself happy, before I met the man of my dreams, someone who treats me very differently to how I had allowed myself to be treated over and over again. When we finally met, it was like the universe hit me over the head with a frying pan. I thought,

'Oh, this is what a relationship should be like. This is the kind of guy I should have been looking for all along. This is the kind of love and life I actually deserve.'

I felt so stupid for the choices I made before, for never opening myself up to someone like him, for allowing myself to believe I deserved anything less, but how could I have known any different? I needed to go through all of those lessons, all of that heartbreak, all of that work, to make me into the version of myself that was able to step into the vibrational frequency that would put me on the same level as the relationship I have now.

For me, I pay attention to lessons that revolve around love, so that's the language the universe uses to talk to me. When my longest relationship broke down, it was the worst thing that ever happened to me. I fell into depression, and I wanted my life, as I knew it, to end. But, the worst time of my life was truly the best thing that ever happened to me, and not just in love.

I climbed up from rock bottom, did the work that I was prompted to do, and changed my life in so many ways. I rose up out of the darkest time in my life, like the lotus flower grows out of dark heavy mud, upgraded my life tenfold, and I'm still learning and doing the work. We all are. The good days and bad days are all temporary, but we're designed to thrive on both.

MONEY

Before you can have the abundance of wealth you asked for, you may have to relearn the value of money. Your

125

childhood beliefs may need to be challenged, you may need to experience the other side of wealth, financial ruin, or struggle, or work harder in order to believe you deserve what it is you want.

You might need to learn how to manage your finances better, and spend less than you earn. The rich stay rich by not spending their money. Millionaires are only millionaires while they have a million in the bank.

You may have some work to do on your self-worth, to realise just how valuable and talented you are, how much you contribute to the world, how much your time and effort is worth, and how much you deserve. This will probably lead you to charge a higher price for whatever it is you do.

Every person's scenario is different. Everyone has their own view of money. Some people need to learn that money isn't evil, and some people need to learn that living like they're loaded, spending cash like there's a hole in their pocket, won't make them rich. The less money you spend, the more money you have.

True wealth is felt through gratitude. Appreciating what you have, recognising that you always have enough, acknowledging that you already have more than you need, and embracing that feeling money gives you, a feeling you already have access to right now, will help you realise that you're already very wealthy.

SUCCESS

Success represents something very different for everyone. The word success could mean almost anything. When you're looking around yourself at people you deem successful, what you don't know is whether their idea of success is the same as yours. It depends on what people want from life, what they feel their purpose to be, how their ideal life looks to them, and who they're comparing themselves to.

On top of that, it is in our nature to move the goalposts every time we achieve a goal. So, the idea of success is individual to each of us, it's fleeting, and it has the ability to make us feel dissatisfied no matter how much we achieve.

You have to find out what success means to you, whether it's wrapped up in a certain amount of money, or leaving a legacy, or creative expression, or making a difference, or having a family, or reaching a particular status in comparison to everyone else. Just remind yourself that no matter where you're at in any moment you are already successful in something, even if that's just surviving this long with what you have and what you know.

What is the feeling you're trying to feel by defining yourself as successful? Do you want to enjoy more time with your loved ones? You have the choice to make that happen now, even in small ways, even just by being more present when you do have the time.

Do you want to enjoy your surroundings, and feel like you live in a luxurious environment? You have the choice to make changes to your environment and experience that now, even just by clearing away the clutter and upgrading your furnishings in small inexpensive ways.

Do you want to feel like you're making a difference, like you're having a positive effect on the people around you? You have the choice to feel that way now, even just by actively listening to your loved ones, helping them in whatever way they ask you to, or by offering to volunteer or get more involved in your community.

NO TWO PATHS ARE THE SAME

There will always be lessons to learn on the way, to your idea of an ideal, abundant life, and all of us have a different way of getting there. No two paths are the same. We are all made of different combinations of experiences, teachings, beliefs, and ingrained psychological issues. To get to where we want to be, we have some work to do on ourselves, each course tailored to our unique individual needs.

This is why you can't achieve the exact same results by mimicking someone else's process. It's also why people achieve things at different stages of their life. For some it comes quickly because they've done a lot of the work already, they know they deserve what they want, and they're putting in the work to get there. For some it comes slowly because they have more to learn, strongly held beliefs that need to be undone, or they've resisted doing any of the work and started later than others.

Don't concern yourself with someone else's journey, focus on yours.

The Law of Attraction is interwoven into the fabric of the universe. It governs our entire experience of life, of reality, of possibility. It's not a separate accessory you can pick up and put down, it's working behind-the-scenes all the time, with or without our supervision. So it's important to consider the bigger picture.

We are each here to experience human life in full, the ups and downs, the lessons and the triumphs, the challenges and momentum of an interesting narrative from birth to death. Although we all long for the ease of instant gratification, of wanting something and just getting it, life would be effectively pointless if we got everything we wanted without anything blocking our path and raising its value. If we were born, got everything we wanted, and then died, would there be any point in being born at all?

Enjoy the process, enjoy the journey. Don't wait to reach the final destination before you allow yourself to be happy. Choose to be happy now, with whatever you have, wherever you are, and wherever you're going.

Choosing to simply change how you feel, every day, to be as happy and as positive as you can, will change your life. You don't even need to apply any kind of process to getting what you want, if you're happy now you already have what you want. The hard evidence that supports your feeling will turn up sooner or later.

So relax. Trust the universe to provide, to hold you and support you, while you follow its guidance to make all your dreams come true.